Lecli

from Andee .

WOMEN ON FIRE

WOMEN ON FIRE

EDITED BY

LORNA KALAW-TIROL

ANVIL

Women on Fire
Lorna Kalaw-Tirol, editor

Copyright © ANVIL PUBLISHING, INC.
and LORNA KALAW-TIROL, 1997

Published and exclusively distributed by
ANVIL PUBLISHING, INC.
3/F Rudgen II Bldg., 17 Shaw Blvd. 1600 Pasig City, Philippines
Telephones: 631-7048, 633-6121, 633-6136
Fax: 631-3766   E-mail: anvil@fc.emc.com.ph

The National Library of the Philippines CIP Data

Recommended entry:

Women on fire / edited by
Lorna Kalaw-Tirol. -
Pasig City : Anvil Pub., c1997
1 v.

1. Women - Philippines - Biography.
2. Philippine essays (English).
I. Tirol, Lorna K.

HQ11123 305.4'092 1997 P972000166
ISBN 971-27-0607-9

Cover art is "House on Fire!" by JULIE LLUCH
(terra cotta, 1991, Ateneo Art Gallery collection)
photographed for Anvil by CHITO MADROÑO and G.K. PANTALEON

Cover and interior design by ANI V. HABÚLAN

Printed in the Philippines by Cacho Hermanos Inc.

*For Gilda Cordero-Fernando,
woman of many passions, guru and friend*

Contents

The Women Behind the Book

Contents

Introduction

"I LOVE your book," said a noted writer when we met shortly after *Coming to Terms* was released in March 1994, "BUT it lacks something. There's no sex! No passion!"

The observation was not a criticism of the women in *Coming to Terms*. I had asked them simply to write about their midlife, a subject Filipino writers had never collectively explored in a book before, and they came up with introspective pieces that inspired Conrado de Quiros to exult, in his Foreword, "Here is nakedness to the marrow of the soul."

A landmark book, the Manila Critics Circle said in citing *Coming to Terms* as the best anthology for 1994. By writing about the realities and possibilities of midlife for women, the writers broke new ground. They were thrilled to be told by complete strangers that the book was helping them to deal with their own midlife and even to enjoy it. Not a few women said they kept their copy of the book on their bedside table and turned to it again and again.

Last year, with *Coming to Terms* going into its third printing and more and more women asking if they could expect a sequel, I felt it was time to go one midlifing step further. I wanted a book that would address the observation the noted writer had made two years before. Maybe this time we could be intimate, as in secrets, not necessarily of the boudoir, but dreams and fantasies, fears and angsts, above all, passions. What are the passions — the forces, the causes, the "special enthusiasms" (to borrow a phrase from life's passages guru Gail Sheehy) — that are driving women in their midlife? And if one of those passions happens to be sexual, how lucky can a book editor get?

That early, I had a title for the new book: *Women on Fire.*

It wasn't easy getting enough women to commit themselves to the kind of book I had in mind. Women of passion, I found out, are inevitably, indubitably, incredibly busy women. They are forever on the move, within the country and outside it — teaching, advocating, lawyering, writing, painting, sculpting, meditating, acting, running a company or an NGO, praying, nurturing, loving. They reminded me of a line from Sheehy's *New Passages:* "That's what passion is all about: allowing yourself to get lost in something."

I had to be patient, and wait.

The final count: eleven essayists and a poet. Each one is a woman I have long admired, in some cases from a distance, for her tremendous intellectual and artistic gifts, her boundless pursuits, her daring spirit, her generous energy.

Marilen Abesamis, my college classmate for two years in the Sixties, was a remarkably sensitive writer even then. She would have gone on to a brilliant career in journalism if a higher cause had not beckoned.

Cristina Jayme Montiel was my student in English composition and literature in her senior year of high school; she edited the school paper and wrote beautiful letters. Today, with a turbulent past behind her and a Ph.D. after her name, she is rediscovering her poetic self.

The Reverend Dr. Elizabeth Tapia I had read about years ago but met only last December at a book launching in which she spoke with such passion of feminism and the spiritual calling.

Many of the writers have more familiar bylines. Barbara (Tweetums) Gonzalez heads a top-rated advertising agency but is better known to readers as the bedimpled woman whose Reality Check column makes the *Philippine Daily Inquirer*'s lifestyle section scintillate on Sundays. Two of her columns are reprinted in this book. Awardwinning essayist and journalist Sylvia L. Mayuga has been scaling mountains, literally and figuratively, since opting to become a fierce advocate for the environment in the Nineties.

Babeth Lolarga will probably be known henceforth as "the country's sexiest poet," all because she dutifully obliged my request for "a sexy and passionate poem."

Julie Lluch is writer and artist both, in each calling exceptional. It is her prized sculpture, "House on Fire," which graces the cover of this book.

Writer and artist, too, plus corporate woman, is Maria Victoria Rufino, whose glamorous photographs in the print media mask a seriousness and depth not usually associated with the social elite.

Boots Anson Roa springs a surprise on those who have boxed her into the Miss Goody-Two-Shoes stereotype, although the wholesome image, her fans should be assured, is intact, and for real.

Narzalina Lim, activist and advocate, was born with a rebellious streak which she explains in an engaging narration of her fascinating family history.

Katrina Legarda underwent a profound conversion between the time she agreed to be a part of this book and the time she was to sit down to finalize her essay. An eleven-year-old girl was raped, allegedly by a member of Congress, and Katrina was asked to help out in the child's fight for justice. The case has changed Katrina's life forever.

Finally, Solita (Winnie) Monsod, whose manuscript, the last to come in, was worth the long months of anxious waiting. Her essay is exuberant, witty and wise as only Winnie Monsod — in advanced middle age, she emphasizes — can be.

So here these 12 remarkable women are, freely and unabashedly writing about the passions that inflame their midlife.

Let them set you ablaze.

Lorna Kalaw-Tirol

Let me thank all the people who made this book possible: Marilen Abesamis, Tweetums Gonzalez, Katrina Legarda, Narz Lim, Julie Lluch, Babeth Lolarga, Sylvia Mayuga, Winnie Monsod, Tina Montiel, Boots Anson Roa, Marivic Rufino and Eliz Tapia; Karina Bolasco and Ani Habúlan of Anvil; Cynthia D. Davila and Josefa R. Curia of Orogem. That we all happen to be women is pure and wonderful serendipity.

Let me also thank Eric Torres of the Ateneo Art Gallery for permission to use Julie Lluch's "House on Fire" on the cover.

My Father's Daughter

MARILEN ABESAMIS

MY FATHER ought to have been a priest, but shortly before he was to have made his vows, my extremely religious grandparents died. And as soon as this happened, he bolted the seminary in search of a wife.

Since my father had something of a healer in him, he chose to be a doctor and later wooed my mother, age 19, at the side of a provincial hospital bed.

My father's religious asceticism and his medical profession combined to make him something of a madman. He was by the door of the church at five in the morning, sometimes before the acolyte was. He walked three miles daily, evidently to unburden—for my mother always teetered on the edge of a breakdown— but to secular friends he said it was great exercise.

For all the walking he did, he needed only two pairs of shoes, carefully chosen from the store Ang Tibay, which lived true to its name. He replaced not the pair, only the soles when the shoes wore thin.

He also had this quirk about entertaining: he forbade us to string festive lights when celebrating a feast or an anniversary, for fear we would unnecessarily hurt the feelings of the needy. As far as I knew, all the neighbors were wealthier than we, so it wasn't clear who it was he feared offending.

So we grew up deeply averse to flaunting but feeling obliged to give, rather generously, because the wealthy-looking people around us might in truth be more needy than we.

Relatives came to be treated for free (and naturally, many claimed to be cured just by the sound of his footsteps at their door). They came back in droves, with other friends, and brought whatever produce they had from the farm. We had plenty of food, but we were often short of cash.

My mother, who was used to a life of wealth and wistfully recounted the horse-drawn carriages of a gilded time, considered him an utter failure. She snubbed my father's relatives, especially those to whom he parcelled some of his inherited land. In the quiet struggle between my mother and my father, I inevitably took my father's side.

We were never poor, and we were never rich either. But because of the battering of "social consciousness" from my father, we found it important to identify with the poor. A preferential option for the poor is how my eldest brother, a Bible scholar, terms it. Meaning, we could have become billionaires — if only we had chosen to do business with the world rather than tried to save it.

MARTIAL LAW hit me when I was aspiring to do my master's and working at a newspaper in New York. When Marcos shut down the media and the international phones, the shock of being unable to communicate with anyone in the homeland, and the imagined horrors of prison and garrison tanks made me crave intensely for home. Suddenly, the avenues and theatres of Manhattan looked so sterile. I wouldn't be found dead in New York! I cried.

Goodbye, Youth! Goodbye, Fun! I was joining the rev, going to a war from which I might never return! I kissed my Jewish boyfriend goodbye, my workaholic deskmate at the office; I also kissed my steadfast one, my Chinese friend who could not see the point of it all. There was no money in a rev.

Even then a political storm was already brewing in the student expat community; so as a fitting despedida to New York, I joined a protest march to the embassy. The embassy staff did not know how to handle the situation: it was the first of a thousand protests that would unfold, but ours was the premiere demo on the East Coast. The US-based personnel, some of them our friends, nervously peered from the upstairs window at the crowd below.

Suddenly, as we sang and cheered, the gates heaved and a mad scramble ensued at the embassy door. I got tossed into the foyer, together with student leaders Ernie Ordoñez and Rom Achacoso. I bit my tongue, dropped the placard "Restore civil liberties!" and came face to face with visiting columnist and joker Joe Guevara. The following morning, our names blazed in the Philippine newspapers and reached my Mom.

My mother was convinced that having thus made it to the national papers as a leader-demonstrator, I had become a Communist in the USA.

"My God, you are now an *atis!*" she cried. Atheist-activist-Communist was what she meant. "Is this true?" she shot at me as soon as I put my luggage down.

"Of course not," I said, but I hardly reassured her. I meant it, but how could she understand? For three months later, I decided to marry the first ex-political prisoner I met — a creature of my mind, a romanticized hero of a relentless, crushing dictatorship.

I entrusted my fate into the hands of this friend, newly delivered from prison, somebody who, I believed, was deeply wounded for his faith and for love of motherland. I worshipped him, mainly because I also wanted so passionately to pay my dues. I felt I had missed out, having so uselessly cavorted and flirted with life on the streets of New York.

Mesmerized, I drew out all my savings from the US and sought his advice on how to spread this wealth. Together, we bought milk for mothers of the poorest prisoners, emptied cabinets for clothes to give the children, and promised jobs to distressed and lonely wives.

Where it was hard to find a job, we harassed friends to create them. Where the women were the no-read, no-write type, we set up our own noodle, pie and pizza shop. The mixed menu showed it wasn't dead serious about profit, but the "feel-good" spirit overflowed.

I thought this was how a real partnership began — one impelled by a vision of a society more equitable and more humane. No matter what objections my mother raised, I insisted I had found my mission — and, how convenient, a bemedaled (meaning tortured) partner to boot.

Then one day, in a voice full of solicitousness and foreboding, my prince said the situation would get "hot" and ex-political prisoners might have to go "underground."

I was not clear what this meant, but it felt like a gun pointed at my neck. I pictured myself abandoned, with my old classmates playing mahjong on weekends, and on workdays, doomed to the ordinariness of writing jingles for bonbons or tampons.

If I clasped him close, I thought, perhaps there would be no such thing as an underground swallowing up those who defied the times. Unabashed, I pressed him to marry me.

A few minutes before the garden wedding I had set (it was too rushed to arrange anything in church), my mother locked me in her embrace, then fell to her knees. "Escape!" she said. My poor mother, who was just beginning to manage on her own six years after my father's death, implored me, "Go! I'll take care of the guests!"

If I was taking on a dictatorship, I didn't realize my mother had been plotting a more dangerous game. She pushed me toward the backdoor, fearing I didn't understand the import of her plea. I blinked, then calmly walked into my Fate.

MY BRIDEGROOM was poor and an anonymous poet, but my mother's instincts were right; he was a gift that was a bit premature. I thought she was railing against the poverty that would soon own me, and against the unorthodoxy that life with an unknown ex-political prisoner spelt.

But I did not wish to wait. Nor did I wish to emulate my aunt who, at 75, eloped to Hawaii with somebody who was running ripe at 85. (My aunt had known her groom all her life. And true enough, with all that wisdom behind her, that relationship lasted till their uneventful deaths, some 12 years later, spiced by occasional fits of jealousy on either side.)

As most everybody knows, people marry for the strangest reasons. Aside from that pure chemical imbalance that sends one's head on a spin, mine included my father's consciousness of the poor, a passion for poetry, and an urgency dictated by the uncertain times.

These reasons did not hold well enough, and after a decade of minor and major surprises, of "fight and flight" marital storms, of peace and belligerence, I became autistic.

I was speechless when I sat at dinner, I always walked three meters ahead of anybody, and I dreaded going home.

I built a world of my own and traveled in an inner landscape that would not unlock. It was only after a full decade that I decided to let go.

The one reassuring space I found throughout the frustrating attempts to rework a disastrous relationship, the one that saved me from myself as I contemplated meeting a truck head-on, or provoking a soldier at a darkened checkpoint, or blowing up a grenade, was service, to people more miserable than myself.

My father would have called it alms, or charity. In my time, it was the pervasive beloved drumbeat: "Serve the people!" Under the threat of death, I had seen many who did it with unflinching grace, who had been witness to deeper tragedies, greater achievements, holier moments. I have seen only a little, very little, but it has given shape to my life.

My bouts with a shaky marriage made me wander from one imaginary oasis to another. I sought an ambiance, a circumstance that would make our union breathe easier, flower even. I was convinced Manila and my clan were too stifling an atmosphere for the rare and delicate breed of love we had. I set sail for the far shores of Mindanao.

(During this time, my Chinese boyfriend came to visit, apparently to snatch me from the dragons of my fate, but since I didn't have a forwarding address and could not be reached, he proposed to a shy and sweet-looking Filipina who happened to sit next to him on his flight back to the US — and he won! He was that good at recovering investments — who can beat the reward of a full-blown wife in exchange for a round trip to Manila?!)

Mindanao then became my home for over seven years, from 1975 to 1982, the years the Marcos military was in constant ascendancy. I joined the nuns who were doing mission for the poor in the war-stricken area, and found the work very therapeutic.

Davao was unlike Manila and more like New York: one could be anything and do anything; one was measured not for the petty and pretty trimmings, but solely for what one was. In the rush of deadlines, one could race out of the house in rubber thongs, unmade-up, and wear one's shirt inside out; the more observant would merely shrug and say, the rich truly have their quirks.

For the nuns took pains to introduce me as "Made in the USA," a woman from a patrician clan, and nothing could make them believe I had been just a clerk among many, in the Land of Plenty.

With our churchworker's salary, the only housing we could afford in Davao was about 30 kilometers from the city center, the roads weaving through thick banana growth. Going out every morning, we bathed in dust and wrapped ourselves in swaths of bandana, *tubao* or netting to keep our heads intact. Coming home on rainy evenings, we clomped through cakes of mud and cow dung. But the air was always sweet and the skies were always naked with stars.

The barrio captain in this little community lived across our house, and we had hardly said hello to his family when he came home dead. He was the head of the notorious Civilian Home Defense Forces (CHDF) and people kept their distance, for the armalites were always slung across his Honda every time he made his rounds. He was killed by the same armalite fire, in mysterious circumstances that no one seemed to want to unravel. Insecurity pervaded the air, an intensity whose memory I still carry to this day.

A few months later, a friend who rushed to the scene of a fire in Agdao's squatter area also met a violent death, killed by the blast of a grenade that had fallen from a soldier's knee. Since we had organized writing seminars together, bantered and spent afternoons just chatting in a stilthouse overlooking the sea, I felt her death very keenly. She could very well have been my child and me.

ANOTHER year later, the Davao cathedral was to be bombed.

It was in the midst of this spiraling violence that I took over the communications desk of the Mindanao Sulu Pastoral Conference, tasked with publishing the church's regional publications.

I started to travel from one end of the island to another. It was an exposure to the poverty of the region and at the same time, to its indescribable wealth.

My job posed a problem that had to be solved if I were to survive in it: that of getting information fast from the width and breadth of the island. In a volatile situation, news meant forestalling disaster or preventing its reoccurrence. But as is often the case with mission work, there was no way we could hire more correspondents or spend more on staff to cover the literally bloody scenes.

There was only one solution: raise the level of literacy and awareness, train those who wanted the skills to create their own beats, write their own stories.

It was a humbling experience. I met people who indeed had very little, yet gave so much, people who received so little, yet appreciated gifts from the heart. A giving society was where we were! Was it despite or because of the red-hot violence and fear that licked at our feet and flowed all around us? Would they have been the grasping, intriguing, loveless characters we see on the front pages today were it not for the crucible of a dictatorship?

We formed a team of journalists and religious in the academe, and together we began to organize workshops on communication skills. We saw teachers, farmers, students, ordinary employees, churchworkers, nuns and seminarians. Invariably, the poorest groups were the most responsive, staying up in seminar halls till the candles flickered out.

Farmers asked hard questions but laughed at jokes so easily the sessions lasted longer than they ought to have. They not only learned to write, they found other mediums of expression which were to them indigenous and hence inexhaustible: songs, cartoons, poetry, drama, anecdotes, narratives — a treasure trove of experiences and ways of doing that was simply amazing.

On the last day of the workshop, we would award prizes to the best pieces. Then we would go to the beach to celebrate, and eat raw fish with *tuba;* we teased one another till tears came to our eyes. Sometimes we would go up the river and into the forest, the boys swinging easily through the trails. Then there were more stories from old faces. More laughter. The smell of coffee made from burnt rice curling, rising, filling us with hope.

One jolly nun who suffered from chronic high blood pressure, like me, found the work therapeutic. She got rid of splitting headaches and palpitation merely by visiting the prison, hugging the old women who needed comforting, and standing up to stiff military men. She said she thought we were giving to the poor, but she felt we were receiving far more. I agreed with her.

Then in 1981 the Vietnam-inspired hamlets began, a strategy that,

Robert McNamara would admit almost two decades after the end of the Vietnam War, was a terrible mistake. The defense secretary of the United States, the mathematical whiz who wanted to manage poverty and solve the world's problems, saw it was not wise to uproot a resilient people. Not all the US-made napalm and the agent orange bombs will make them give up their land.

It was Christmas 1981, a mysterious time. In the Davao provinces, knocks on housegates were reported being heard at night. Shots at checkpoints. Salvaged bodies at the cogon clumps near the seminary. Fear intensified as each embellished story made the rounds.

The center of military anger was Laac, a town of Davao Norte province, where an army commander said, "Laac is a beautiful lake, in which there are some bad fish." To catch the bad fish, the soldiers were told, "it is necessary to drain the lake."

Thousands of families were then ordered by the military to dismantle and abandon their farmhouses in the countryside, and to move into the barrio and town centers several kilometers from their farms. In January, some 70 "strategic hamlets" were created in Davao and the surrounding barrios of adjacent Agusan.

The most striking pictures I have left of that experience were taken by a cripple, a magnificent friend whose eyes were as sharp as his mind. They show the faces of women and old men framed in the tight slats of chicken coops, their legs dangling in space. They show backs bent from carrying dismembered posts of dwellings, and frail children following in their trail.

The cherished eagle, according to a popular song, had fled Davao, as did the native people who had the option: they sailed to Cebu or anywhere far. But for those who had not much choice, they had to be malleable, their anger muted and their muscles stretched so they could think far, far beyond the present.

I saw a woman who died while fleeing. Her family did not have time to bury her; they could not leave her either, so they carried her on a sled. They dragged the sled down to the barrio chapel, where they hoped they could have a proper wake. But the chapel was full with the living, huddled and sleeping in the only preserved structure around.

Behind the chapel, another woman was being comforted by her husband. Her moment had come, and she gave birth to a son.

Everywhere, women were cuddling their frightened children or stroking the heads buried in their breasts.

As I lay on the wooden bench in the chapel to get some rest that night, I felt very close to these strangers around me, as if we were soon to meet a common fate. The petromax beaming from the soldiers' out towers and the candles on the altar threw light on the faces of the refugees that made them look solemn in their giving and eternal in their faith.

In a corner, a child was whispering a Christmas song, her eyes squeezed tight.

It was the holiest Christmas I have ever had.

Did I feel it intensely because in that eerie environment women stood out as helpless victims of a very dominating, unbending military policy? Did I see death and wish for mine?

So it was for a long time that Davao communities continued to be torn apart, and we who were only minimally affected nursed a hopelessness and fear that this was not to be the end, but only the beginning of a bigger war.

Then slowly reports came in from the barrios, from all affected areas (in the form of anecdotes, cartoons, poetry, a listing of facts). The national and international media focused on the human suffering, picked up the senselessness and the viciousness of the military strategy.

Though it seemed such a long time, the hamlets were eventually dismantled. But in my own home front, the situation deteriorated very fast.

IT WAS 1982. My husband Joe and I now managed to take diametrically opposed positions on every issue under the sun. If he said he liked blue, I would prefer yellow. If he said "No" to an invitation, I'd say "Sure!" If he said Ninoy had collapsed, I would first verify. I became much more belligerent.

On more conciliatory evenings, we would walk to the *panciteria* for a weekend treat. Once we were seated, the dialogue would unfold so:

Waiter, pencil on pad, starts blinking his eyes.

Joe orders. He doesn't ask me.

"One order of *pancit,* one order of sweet-and-sour pork, and one *lumpia.* That's it," he says, smiling.

The waiter looks at me. "Your drink, Ma'am?"

Joe jumps in his seat. "Oh, and plain rice, don't forget. Drinks? Coke for me and 7-up for her."

"Beer," I say. I want something strong.

"Shouldn't you just have a soft drink?" Joe suggests. Coke is sharp, 7-Up is docile and beer is out of the question.

"No, I want beer." I look the waiter straight in the eye.

"Soft drink," Joe smiling, holds the waiter's arm. It is final.

I would feign dizziness and refuse to eat. We would take out the leftover when he was done.

There would be more war scenes, then he would write poetry, his way of saying "Sorry." There would be a tentative silence, then another cycle of confrontation and peace. When the cycles came in quick succession, I was ready to call it quits.

Four months pregnant, I left Mindanao for the US, with no one knowing about the movements inside my body except my mother.

I knew that from afar there would still be occasion to press for political freedom, but I was going to fight desperately for my personal one.

I went back to New York and in that familiar territory coaxed kind memories to stroke the abandoned child in me. I plumbed the streets of Chinatown for my favorite Szechuan food, walked through Central Park where my friend and I used to bike in tandem, bought bags of delicious chestnuts and threw them at the swans. My self-confidence had plummeted to zero; I felt like a candle being eaten up. For the first time, I consciously indulged myself. I was grieving and deserved empowering, anything. In my less desperate moments, my other self would remonstrate, what was my misery compared to where a thousand others had been?

What greatly lightened my burden was the presence of a kindly cousin in New York who took me in and later introduced me to an OB-Gyne who was ready to assist at childbirth a Filipina who didn't have money to pay. Dr. Elena Basa welcomed strangers, made me feel easy about myself. She discussed the possibility of my giving birth in my cousin's kitchen, anywhere I felt comfortable in. She was lovely, and game.

But when the moment came, it was not without its trauma. Fortunately, I had come to know that a human being is infinitely malleable and adaptable. "It's all in the mind," I intoned the mantra. I was dough that could be pressed and kneaded, thrown up and slapped on the tiles and still be dough. Still in one piece.

My cousin left for a Christmas reunion with family in Manila. She had hoped I could still hold off till she got back. But five days before Christmas, the baby started to roll.

I took a taxi to the hospital after bidding my nine-year-old daughter, my truest companion, to prepare our room and the diapers. It was something she performed with great anticipation. The baby, after all, was to be our Christmas present to each other.

The cab driver must have sensed that I was going to burst at any moment and mess up the inside of his cab. So he swerved in the direction of a hospital which was nearest the freeway exit but not where my doctor was. I grabbed his neck. "Please," I said, "I have no insurance. Take me to the right hospital, where I can have a safe delivery."

It took him forever to find it, and by the time he screeched to the door of the right hospital, my tummy was almost gone. I snatched the arm of a running wheelchair, grateful for this bit of high-tech. But as soon as I stripped to lie naked on the ER table, I clearly sensed trouble.

"Oh my gosh! Holy cow!"

"Is this AIDS!?" the student nurses yakked.

I had contracted the American strain of chicken pox three weeks before and the blotches were still red on my skin. Never mind if the head of the baby was already in my palm, the medical people fled.

My doctor came and calmed the crazy staff, but I was nevertheless barred from the delivery room. If I still had the pox virus, the hospital said, I would contaminate the next generation of Americans now struggling at birth. So with God and my doctor as witnesses, in a hall outside the delivery room, I did it the most natural way (sans anesthesia, sans medical paraphernalia, sans music that they say gets piped into delivery rooms).

Well, my second daughter was born complete, with no pox on her head. I then reflected on my blessings: yes! 1) I was alive all these 36 years! 2) free at last from a failed marriage, and 3) held the gift of a baby! I thought I could spend the whole night like this, in an outpouring of gratitude.

That was not to be.

My first impulse of fear came when I felt a twitch on my side. I yanked the bell but no one came. I screamed, but no one seemed to hear. Meanwhile, out of the corner of my eye, I saw the procession of men and women in white flowing along the banks of the corridor, but no one so much as peeked in on me.

By the time I sorely needed the bedpan, I knew it was a hopeless situation. It was the pox! I could burst my appendix, die, and no one would know. It was worse than being deserted in the dark hills of Laac.

So I squinted, crawled out of bed, dextrose dangling from my arm, crawled to the corner table where I thought the bedpan must be. But if it wasn't?

In those few minutes of desperate search, I felt very lonely. How I longed for the smell of burnt-rice coffee, for the warmth of the humble farmhouse of Davao! All the high-tech in this now glitzy megacity called Big Apple could not provide me the simplest prop for my most shrieking basic need.

Finally, in the shadows of that dumb room, I clutched at the rim of the bedpan. It was like striking gold! Dignity forbade me to do on the floor what I freaking needed to do, so I dutifully crawled back. I squinted, concentrated on the glint of steel that held the bedpost. Wow! I lifted the sheets and prayed.

I emptied myself with both pain and joy, then floated. When I next opened my eyes, the rays of the winter sun were stealing into the glass doors. It was 8:00 a.m. I had checked in shortly after midnight, and gazed at my baby at 2:00 a.m. It was December 21, two days short of my father's birthday.

Cheered, I decided to get up and go.

I NAMED my daughter after women friends who had sailed on the MV Cassandra in November 1982, but never made it to the retreat house they were headed for in Cebu.

Sisters Nanette, Amparo, Consuelo and Concepcion were among the people I had worked with in the communities of Davao and with whom I had frequently taken trips, sometimes down the Agusan River, at other times on unpaved paths to tribal folk and Muslim settlements.

On the hour they sailed, the clouds threatened a squall, but the captain decided it was going to be fine. As the ship combed the tricky Surigao Straits, the vessel started to keel. Water poured into the cabins and roared onto the floor. The sisters stopped the crew, who replied that there was nothing to worry about. It turned out they were already racing down the ladders and abandoning ship.

As some of the two hundred survivors would later recount, the sisters and other church people brought down the life vests and organized the lowering of the boats. They helped the women and children don their safety jackets. Then they held hands, formed a circle and knelt as the ship went down.

These were the spirits I called forth the second time I checked in, when my infant daughter lay dying in the hospital. We were in the ICU, not knowing what the matter was, except that the drugs wouldn't work. My baby was convulsing the whole day and the whole night.

How does a mother feel about the impending loss of a child that is inevitably her last? How does one stop blaming oneself for something as terrible as a fall that one did not see?

Between the doctor's initial warning ("I don't think she will make it," she said) and her depressing "we cannot tell you what functions she has lost" were two weeks of nerve-wracking vigil. I talked to Anna every minute of my waking hour. I refused to leave the ICU despite the rules, and the nursing staff no longer bothered for they were convinced by then that I had become crazed.

The accident happened during one of those nights I was out with American friends who were gripped by events in the Philippines and wanted to contribute their bit by pondering, writing, speaking and petitioning US lawmakers to end support to Marcos.

Ninoy's death on the airport tarmac shocked the expatriate community as much as the locals, pushing even the traditionally apolitical groups to unprecedented action. Talk shows, pickets, press conferences, fund-raising activities dovetailed with one another. A thousand ideas flew like confetti on our lives, and they all needed to be worked on and done.

While I was at one such conference, a young kid in the household snuck into our bed, held the baby and accidentally dropped her. It was only after we had emerged from the hospital ICU that I was told what had actually transpired.

I think midlife crisis is when your past life flashes in your mind and, terribly tired, you decide it is not worth carrying on with the other half. I had forgotten how to smile. I just wanted to bury myself somewhere deep, where nobody would detect, waken, or accuse me of my life's biggest failures.

On the day my baby regained color and fluttered her eyes, I was half-dead. Having cajoled her while she convulsed, talked to her through the haze, baptized her immobile body, stroked her wounded head and limbs for a fortnight, I now needed almost an act of faith to believe she had come back.

She revived, but the doctor said I should keep watching for signs. It was at this point that I marked my midlife.

I'd been given a second chance! I promised I'd carry on, better, higher ... I still didn't know how and where exactly, but I promised.

IN FEBRUARY 1986, when the stark image of Marcos flashed on the TV screen, surrounded by his beleaguered family and framed by dark, ornate drapes, I knew that soon it would be time to go home. We disposed of the house, whipped its meager contents into *balikbayan* boxes and thrilled at the prospect of going home, hopefully for good.

At this point, it might be useful to say that people like me who had dreamt of a better society and had given all to see its coming, can never have an easy time adjusting. Especially to a situation that didn't turn out as they had expected it to be.

There are those who hanker for the old enemies, and can't rest; sometimes they create enemies out of friends. There are those who still hold on to old maps, when the ground beneath them has already swelled, huge islands have been swallowed up and new rock formations have surfaced. They believe the Nineties are just the flipside of the Sixties.

And there are those who, deeply chastened, work at a more humble present, awaiting the new order, in whatever shape it will come.

For both, the hopes are tempered. In the change of seasons, no one hazards the old fearless forecasts. It is a complex time.

We know it is the end of the Cold War, the end of reason, the end of nature even (note the splitting of genes so that human growth hormones can become soul to the pig or the blue tomato). But what is it a start of? Globalization? Web Information Revolution? Feminization? Spiritualization? The –isms are out, the –ations are in. It is definitely a transition period.

What to do during "waiting time"? I could, finally, go back to school as a number of friends have done (reclaim their MAs and PhDs or just go on a mental sabbatical, an "emptying" so the good wine can flow easy). I could find me a sugardaddy.

I chose to be an entrepreneur. Having seen so much poverty, I could now use a lot of money.

I dreamt of a funding agency that would provide decent people with funds without having to seek assistance from abroad. I wanted to save Laguna de Bay (Ming Ramos beat me to the Pasig). I planned a halfway house that would take in people in trauma, a school for wounded people who want to get back on track, etc. I had a hundred and one things on the agenda.

But first I had to find that million.

So I sought a friend who owned a poultry farm and bargained her down. I got chicken on credit, then dressed and sold them in parts or whole, intact or deboned, and talked people into cutting cholesterol. "Go for chicken!" was my new battle cry.

Before the year was over, my poultry magnate friend tired of traffic, tired of commuting to her farm. She closed shop and I had to look for other sources, only to discover, at every end, the hand of the cartel.

So I turned to fish. Sighting an old piece of property near Laguna de Bay, I built a fishpen. Then officials at the Laguna Lake Development Authority (LLDA) said the water is dying and it will take years to detoxify. The only silver lining writ on the once pristine waters (the very same bay that Jose Rizal, while in Switzerland, said was beautiful beyond compare) is that the murk beneath the fishpens might someday jell into solid real estate. Like a blessing, the storm blew my pen away, and I didn't need to worry about what to do with the water.

Obviously, I haven't made my million, but I think I've made some progress. I'm now packing organic fertilizer extracted from the essence of chicken feathers and fishtails.

My business is exceedingly small, but my brother says I run it like a multinational. That's because I sit and facilitate at staff meetings, asking my driver and my maids to solve our current problems. They discuss, then decide on how things should be done; they debate on whom to hire and fire; they decide on whom to serve and which day to serve customers. They vote on plans; they veto some.

"I read in today's papers," one of my maids said, "that somebody committed suicide because of chicken sausages."

"They tried so hard, but they owed so much to the bank!" said another. So we held off on such plans.

I tell them the success of the venture is in their hands and they should quit if they're not having fun. They sing and laugh while working. I don't mind; in fact, I'm happiest when the kitchen hums. Some boys I've fired and surprisingly they try to reform, cry to be taken back.

I TELL my children the secret of life is in relationships. One doesn't need all that money. My children insist they want both to have money and to be happy. Having been knocked around a bit, they have no illusions life will be easy. I trust that they, who are my greatest gifts, will grow up okay and will know how to handle life, the tough parts as well as the sweet.

Unselfishly, they have given their blessings to a stepfather who followed us home from the US. They care for him, and they genuinely like him, for we live apart most of the time. (My husband swears this is the secret of a relationship: not to work nor to love in such close quarters.) My children and I are in Manila, and he is often in outer space.

Sometimes, as a blended family, we visit the grave of my father and tell him we have all connected. That his impulse lives on, even in midlife, and will probably not be exhausted soon.

Just Four More Sleeps

BARBARA C. GONZALEZ

FOUR MORE sleeps and it's going to be my birthday!

Are you appalled that a woman my age — I'm turning 52 — is so excited about a birthday? It is shocking even to me. The last time I celebrated was in 1988, when it was the year's most coveted date: 8-8-88. Pregnant women everywhere were having births induced so they could have babies on this lucky date.

I was born on 8-8-44, and turned 44 in '88. There's symmetry to my aging. I turn a double-number age in a double-number year. In 1977, I was 33. In 1999, I will be 55. So we had a party and never again since.

I got stuck in a warp of the spirit. I began to get depressed about getting older. I got into a what's-there-to-celebrate mode. Thankfully, family and friends never leave me alone. They indulge my negativity and drag me through a birthday bacchanal that lasts at least a week.

"How old are you?" someone asked two years ago.

"F-f-f-ff...," I tried to answer, but turned blue instead.

"Give yourself time," older friends advised. "You'll get used to it."

It took maybe six months to get used to being 50, and another six months to realize that this is a great age to be. It should be written about so those approaching what they call the "golden years" don't do so with the terror I did.

If we assume an 80-year life span, then 40 years would be midpoint. Once you hit 50s, downward slide is implied, since old age is often described as a "second childhood."

So, if you ignore physical aging — and believe me, it's worth ignoring

— and just look at your psychological profile, then you know that at 50 you begin to "youthen." You hit that F-f-fff wall and suddenly the F word means free to finally be whatever fits your fancy.

The kids are old and settled. I ask my 30-something kids whose children they are. They're too old to be mine. I feel their age but I'm less conservative and constrained. They're still trying to please other people while I am learning to please myself.

Life is now refreshingly simple. Money is not a problem, not because I have it but because I know how to raise what I need. The purest joy comes from the smallest things: a whole weekend with nothing to do; a dress that still fits after all these years; friendships new and old; a good book. I no longer worry about external things.

Instead, I spend time exploring the mysterious caves of my much-neglected soul. How do I really feel? For the first 40 years, we seem to search for identity, who we are in the outside world. Fr the next 40 years — possibly less, but plenty of time, anyway — we search for authenticity, who we are inside.

What do I really feel like doing? Dancing? With a paid dancing instructor (DI) at a ballroom-dancing place? I sweep up my baby grandson who presses his chubby cheek against mine as I whirl him around the room in a clumsy tango, until we both collapse from giggles and chuckles. Maybe I'll graduate to DIs. Maybe I won't. It all depends on how I feel.

The high of being 50 is experiencing personal growth and realizing that it's not too late for anything. The high of being 50 is seeing that life is changed but still worth living. There's hell to raise — and you can raise it better from an authoritative age — some promises to keep and miles to go . . . beyond four more sleeps.

And if one fine morning you fail to wake, hey, it was fun, wasn't it? You won't know what it feels like to be fitted into a coffin, so why worry?

At this late age, I realize that the bloom is not off the rose. But the rose is in me, in a secluded soul glen, in my own secret garden.

Perhaps what I want to say is best distilled by a conversation my daughter Sam and I had about Rodin, who said all creative power is sexual. Sam thought it was the sculptor's excuse for promiscuity.

I didn't want to pass judgment on poor dead Rodin, so I told her what I've come to know: at my age what is most potent is creative power, and sexual power is just one aspect of that. The word *libido*, I have come to realize, expands at this age to embrace how you feel about all of life. In youth, I just referred to sexual power, a limited definition, that led to contraction and not expansion.

If you are open to it, ferocious creative power can come with being

50. It's the age when you consider all the other things you want to do and go for them. It is a bold, fearless, magical age where your only limit is your imagination. That's why it's worth celebrating.

That's why I'm leading the celebrations this year. I am glad I was born. I am happy to be alive. I am celebrating my birthday. Just four more "sleeps" and I'll be 52. Isn't that something?

The Return of the Bod

LAST WEEK'S column ended with a personal classified ad simply because it seemed a good way to end the piece.

Oh, come on. Maybe I really wanted to know what would happen if I put myself on the marriage market.

I found out. I was barraged with mail — from women who really enjoyed the pointers on brain exercise. Not a single marriage proposal.

Reality was checked. No one wants to marry an old challenging mind. On the marriage market, it's body that counts.

Who dares deny that, in what pundits (and I write that with contempt) call the "golden years," the mind may scintillate, the spirit may soar, but the body just goes — precisely why in the golden years we exercise our minds (they respond); we stimulate our spirits (to fly us into the next frontier beyond this life); and we view our bodies with not just a grain of salt but very salty humor.

WHEN I was 16, I had what young people now call "a bod," and I therefore had my own stable of suitors,

One, who was quite aggressive and manipulative, was also very frustrated when I categorically said I didn't much like him. But suitors then and now had many strategies, and he managed to get my mother to invite him and his cousins to our farm. I wasn't crazy about the idea, but figured that if his cousins were there, it wouldn't be so bad. I rather liked his relatives.

On the scheduled day, he showed up bogged down by a straw hat, transistor radio and camera. He looked like a tourist just off the boat. A 16-year-old with a bod does not like this.

To make matters worse, his cousins never showed up, and we went to our farm just with him. I was on my worst behavior. Then and now, I didn't like being deceived.

By the end of the day, he had had it with me and I had had it with him. As I walked ahead of him to the car, he swung his camera at my derriere (that's French for what Americans call "buns"). I guess he wanted my attention.

Enraged, I turned on him and said. "Do that again, and I'll throw your camera to the fields."

He smiled, an irritating I-love-it-when-you're-angry grin. He did it again. Offended, defiled, arrogant as only a 16-year-old with a good bod can be, I grabbed the camera and threw it away.

LIFE happened. Years passed. I got my comeuppance. I aged. I lost my great bod to four children and food.

What body I had left could still pour into tight-fitting jeans, which I wore because they made me feel funky. I didn't get rave reviews. Maybe my friends, who were Filipinos, just didn't feel it was important to tell me how they thought I looked in jeans. Or maybe they were afraid to, because I was already training for Dragon Lady. Maybe I intimidated them.

We were visiting New Orleans. It was evening and I was dragging behind my friends, trying to disguise my disappointment.

I wanted to have dinner at one of the chic restaurants (I'm the type who would blow three days' budget on one elegant dinner that includes champagne and a soufflé Grand Marnier). They wanted to eat at a cheap place and had headed off to look for one. I, sulking in protest, lagged behind.

Suddenly, the earth shook. I was jolted. It took a few seconds to realize what had happened. Someone had just whacked my derriere.

I looked behind me. Walking away, flanked by two laughing buddies, was a towering redneck in leather motorcycle vest, greasy blond hair down to his shoulders. He didn't break his pace. Laughing, he called back, "Great butt!"

I was stunned. There is still a prudish Filipina who lives in me, even if I try to hide her with dragon-lady language. Then I realized I had just turned 40. "Not bad for a 40-year-old," I grinned.

What age can do to us! How it can change our view of the world. I was actually flattered. I felt, well, so sexy.

YESTERDAY, I forgot I was going to a construction site first thing in the morning. I only remembered I was going to dinner last thing at night.

Thanks to today's engineering, I can still wear miniskirts and a decolletage without being visually offensive. So, all dressed up for a casual dinner, I walked through the construction site in a miniskirt and decolletage.

Sure, I had a blazer on, but that just gave the construction workers something to peep into. Those who weren't into bosoms not very discreetly stared at my legs.

I was initially uncomfortable. This was stupid of me. I should have dressed more appropriately. How could I have forgotten? I must be getting really old. I forget too much too often.

Then I realized the guys sneaking a look at my cleavage and legs were in their twenties and thirties. Thank you, guys, look all you want. Liberated, I concentrated on not falling. I mean, that would have really damaged me. My legs might look good but my bones are probably brittle. It would take longer to heal a fracture at this age.

See, keeping the mind exercised can help the body somewhat.

You know support hose will work wonders on your legs, and you know where to buy the best. You know underwires will hold up anything, and you know exactly what brand works for you. You know the difference between the fool (the one who wears a mini to a construction site) and the fooled (20-year-olds who ogle legs half as old as century eggs). You know it's great to be a funny old fool with a sharp mind and great legs.

Hey, I didn't say it. They said it. I'm just translating for them. I just told them how old I was, and they were too embarrassed to speak.

Reprinted from her column, Reality Check,
Philippine Daily Inquirer

The Law Above All

KATRINA LEGARDA

I REMEMBER the first time I met the child. September 15, 1996. It was the day after June Ambrosio came to my house and begged me to help her with the case. She said to me, "Look at your daughter tonight and imagine that she is sleeping next to this congressman. Tell me you won't take the case."

The girl is very pretty, with little dimples and very long hair. We spoke to her for four hours. She was very open when she talked about school, movies, friends, books. But when we came to the abuse, her face closed down and her eyes became dull and she started speaking in a very low voice. She was diffident about talking about what happened to her. Who can blame her? She had been given the run-around by people in government and so was very wary and distrustful of everyone. Of course you come to her thinking that at age 11 she could have been trained by someone, but I have spoken to her 25 times since September 15 and she has not changed her story. I guess it is the truth.

Sometimes I have regretted saying yes to the case. My time is no longer mine and I have had to fight so many people to protect this one child. I feel like I'm burning so many bridges for her. But in fact it does not really matter if I do not practise law anymore after this case. I want to prove a point — that nobody, I don't care who you are, must be above the law.

It is the passion of my life right now. In fact it is the passion all three of us women lawyers on the case against Romeo Jalosjos share. We want to put this man in jail. The fate of this child rape victim has made me realize that children have no one to protect them. Children without parents, and even children with parents, have no one to protect them when it comes to adults who are exploiting them. I had known about child abuse and child exploitation and child prostitution, but I had thought that as a general rule they happened among the uneducated. Only foreigners bought Filipino children, or so I thought. It never occurred to me that even lawmakers buy children. I thought that with their money and power and influence they did not have to buy women — women would flock to them on their own. That was what disturbed me most about the case.

Before this child came along, I had been handling the cases of adult women. How I got into that kind of lawyering is a story in itself.

WHEN I withdrew from the partnership at the giant firm ACCRALAW and set up a tiny law office with a friend, my only hope was to keep myself and my children above water, but independent. Suddenly, I found myself listening to the miseries and problems of women, and blazing into the public eye.

I have never thought of myself as someone particularly sympathetic to people who harbor angst in their personal relationships. I have always felt that if you're not happy, then perhaps you should just get out of the particular hole in which you happen to be that is causing all the unhappiness or at least standing in the way of your personal search for internal bliss.And so, when after 12 years as a student in England my mother forced me into the study of law, I felt removed from those aspects which required understanding of, empathy and sympathy for a client's personal affairs of the heart.

Sure enough, when I was accepted in the Angara Abello Concepcion Regala and Cruz Law Firm as an associate 16 years ago, I was marked for, and eventually assigned to, corporate litigation. In that field you examine the loopholes of corporate lawyers and, on those bases, attempt to win in behalf of the faceless and soulless client thousands or even millions of pesos in damages. You are safe in the knowledge that the only thing your client can lose is property. You do not worry about his/her private life or children or even his/her state of mind. You do not have sleepless nights dreaming of children screaming as they are torn away from the hapless arms of their helpless (read: poor) mothers. You do not have pangs of guilt as you agonize over a father's rights to visit, to love or to embrace his innocent children.

Then, like a lightning bolt, I was "adopted" by some politicians who were my mentors and led into a path from which I could not turn back. They asked me to run for the Senate. Traveling through the country for the senatorial campaign made me open my eyes and realize that out there is the real world — a world which is not wrapped in the protective cocoon of an air-conditioned, carpeted, hushed and well-staffed office. Out there was Reality. Men toiling to feed their large broods. Women suffering from each thoughtless delivery of a child. Children grubbing in the dumps for scraps to sell or exchange in hopes of a better life. Worse, I met well-meaning matrons urging educated women to teach others their "rights." And I laughed.

What rights? The laws are there, to be implemented only if the person who seeks protection has money, connections or some other wherewithal. But how can you tell a woman living in the boondocks of the Cordillera that she can escape the beatings of an abusive husband by just walking out? Where would she go?What would she do to earn a living? And who, in the meantime, would take care of all her children?

I knew then that I could not, in conscience, stay within the confines of my safe and protected environment. I knew that the steady income I was receiving would not assuage the strength of the surprising feelings that emanated from within me. And I left, with fingers crossed and with the best (if idealistic) of all intentions. I did not really know how or where to start. But I believed that Somebody out there or up there wanted me to "do something."

In the meantime, I also left my marriage. It was a marriage which I felt had collapsed soon after the birth of my second child, but to which I clung as an anchor against the devastating grief brought on by the twin sudden deaths of my sister and my mother. As I recovered from my sorrow, I discovered within me the strength to walk out of a marriage which was not making me grow, was not supportive of my strong desire to help people, and was a manifestation of everything my grandmother said was wrong in male-female relationships.

Then, about three months after I had left my marriage and organized this tiny law office, Jullie Yap Daza calle... One of the guests invited to her television show (a woman lawyer, I understand) backed out at the last minute. Jullie asked me, frantically, if I could take the lady's place. The topic was annulment and divorce, about which I knew very little. At that time, the Family Code was very new and was not the law I had studied in school or for the bar. "Never mind," Jullie urged, "you can read and then you can waffle through." OK. After all, waffling was one of my greatest gifts, according to a tutor of mine at university in Britain.

I do not know how I conducted myself on that show. I do not know how I came across to the audience. I was not used to television cameras. And I certainly was not used to talking about my thoughts in public. But after that night, my office was inundated with calls from women begging my help to rid them of their abusive, controlling, or even inconvenient husbands. I found myself inundated with work, speaking engagements and a feeling of helplessness as I tried to understand, empathize and sympathize with so many unhappy people.

The first thing I realized was that taking on the mantle of a "family law lawyer" was much more difficult than battling in court with the counsel of those faceless corporations. I had to learn not only what the law is on the family, but also to understand the emotions and the psyche of the men and women who came to me for help. I had to take up the cudgels for the innocent children caught in the middle of their parents' war, and be the lawyer for those children who would otherwise not be protected, as their parents were merely using them as a battleground, uncaring of their feelings and desires. My own personal experiences turned out to be extremely helpful in all these matters.

Many women lawyers are doing annulment and separation cases now. I'm not so sure they give the kind of pragmatic advice I give; maybe they just stick to the law. I don't take a case unless I know a woman is absolutely ready to go to court. When a woman comes to me, I warn her that if she wants to leave her husband she has to be aware that her economic situation will suffer, especially if she has no income of her own. And she has to worry about what people will say to her and about her. There are many groups in society that still consider separated women pariahs.

You know, the law covers a vast spectrum of our personal lives. The law tells us when we can marry and how we should marry. The law tells us the grounds upon which we can seek escape from the marriage we thought would last forever, as taught to us by our Catholic schools. The law tells us about children — who are legitimate and who are not, who has parental authority over them, who has custody, what names they should take and how much they are entitled to as support and inheritance. The law tells us what we can and cannot do while we are married. It even tells us that our society recognizes and accepts the Filipino male trait of entering into illegitimate and immoral relationships. The law gives those resulting mistresses the right to claim a certain portion of the properties which they acquired together with other women's husbands.

In fact, I might as well inform you, if you do not know it yet, that today a pregnant 16-year-old girl cannot marry her boyfriend, nor can the boyfriend be forced to marry her. Such a marriage is void, even if both parents have given it their consent. Thus, the law impliedly urges us to teach morality and, if morality is not available, then to teach about birth control. This is good, and fair to all the teenagers out there who watch our lousy local movies and learn the execrable values portrayed in them. We must begin to teach in the home. We must address the important issues of sex and sexuality with candor and openness. We must stop hiding behind our so-called Catholic faith, because it is instituting a society of illegitimate relationships and bastards.

The law has been tempered by the recognition of a foreign divorce decree. This means that if a foreigner initiates and secures a foreign divorce decree against his or her Filipino spouse, the divorce is recognized in the Philippines and the Filipino is deemed single and capacitated to remarry. This is a great deliverance to all those Filipino women who, having married and been divorced from foreign spouses, have had to live "in sin" since their long-ago divorces.

Better yet, our law has finally recognized that some people should simply not have married each other. A provision which acts as our Philippine Divorce Law tells us that if one spouse should be found to be "psychologically incapacitated" to comply with his/her marital obligations, then the other spouse may seek a declaration of nullity of the marriage. Their children remain legitimate, but it is as if the couple had never married. (A throwback to our faith whereby divine mistakes are not recognized.)

I remember the first case we ever handled. It was a custody problem. The woman— I'll call her Tina — was an intelligent, if hysterical, professional whose lawyer had so mishandled her case that her three-year-old son was placed by the court in the joint custody of his parents. Under the law, a child seven years of age and below cannot be taken away from his mother, unless there is a compelling reason such as a communicable disease or the mother is living with a man not her husband. (Morals, morals, dear people.) We sent Tina to a child psychologist who discovered that her son was badly disturbed every time he returned from his father's home. On the basis of the psychologist's report, we were able to persuade the court to change its order and return the child to his mother's full-time custody, allowing the father only visitorial rights. In the beginning, Tina did not want her husband to have the right to even see his son. She hated her husband and wanted to "teach him a lesson." We told her that unfortunately, for the rest of his life, her husband would be the father of her son and that depriving a child of his father's love, care and attention would be so detrimental to his psyche that all his future adult relationships may well be affected. Anyway, all ended well. Hopefully, Tina's son will grow up to be a kind and concerned person, with the ability to love and care for another human being. Sometimes I wonder whether children used as battlegrounds ever rid themselves of the scars.

Our clients belong to all socio-economic classes. We meet with the very rich as well as truly impoverished women who defied their upbringing and values and lived in with men who were married to other women. It is the poor who are stronger, I guess because of the adversities they have gone through. Many rich women, on the other hand, come and tell me they want me to go to court to force their husbands to love them again. That's bloody ridiculous! I tell them they don't need a lawyer. Love is something you can't just demand. The poor, on the other hand, don't talk about love, they talk about support and peace of mind. In some of their cases, though, I have found myself helpless. I cannot afford to go out of town on my own resources. I have children to feed, an office to maintain, staff to pay. At times, the only thing I can do is refer poor clients to an office of legal aid which may have the funding to take on cases like theirs.

Then, too, we meet with men and women who are simply tired of their spouses. Tired of fighting over petty things. Tired of the sexual infidelities, of the lies and the misery of just living day to day with a person they cannot stand to look at anymore. These people have no recourse in the law. They do not have true grounds for annulling their marriages. For these people, again, we are sometimes helpless. We have to advise them to seek psychological counseling to discover whether there is something more within the marriage and the feelings engendered by that marriage which could allow a declaration of its nullity. For these people, I long for the passage of a decent, dignified and humane Divorce Law.

It really bothers me that, because of the Catholic Church's hold on our society and on those whom we elect to govern us, we cannot allow our people to exit gracefully from a very human error of having chosen a mate who they believed would be a mate for life. We are not God. We must admit to human error. We must recognize that a marriage was celebrated before God. But here we are, blindly pursuing the tenet that what God has put together, no man can put asunder.

I realize that God is all-knowing. I was taught that God does not make mistakes. But I was also taught that God gave us free will. And it is in the exercise of that free will that we choose our partners in life for the procreation of the children who will continue to people the earth. Where is the divinity in that choice? Did God come to us in our dreams and tell us whom to choose? I don't think so. Did God create us all to be good, loving and responsible people who, once we have married, will no longer look at another of the opposite (or even of the same) sex? Persons who will work hard to support our families in the best possible way? Persons who did not invent drugs or alcohol or even persons who do not indulge in the physical abuse of other human beings?

So why do we ignore these human frailties? Why do we insist on following the Catholic teaching that a marriage must be as if it had never existed if there is a flaw in its execution or consummation? Why do we ignore that there are children who emanate from these marriages? That there are properties which are acquired? That there are relationships forged as a result of a marriage?

I don't know, and I am fighting what seems to be a lonely battle for the passage of a divorce law which will give all our unhappy men and women the right to live happy lives once again. I am not even asking for a divorce law which would enable couples to uncouple "without fault" on either side. I am merely asking for a law which would allow men and women to return to that good night of singlehood with dignity and grace. I don't mind if somebody has to be at fault. I do mind, however, that under our present law the "innocent" can no longer be supported by the guilty. You may not be aware that when a marriage has been declared null and void, neither party is obliged to support the other anymore. And why not? Because it is as if there was never a marriage. The marriage is not recognized anymore, and all the obligations and responsibilities which sprang from it are no longer supposed to exist. But the fact is they do continue to exist even after the court order has been rendered, and we are hypocrites if we continue to allow ourselves to be blinded by our adherence to our faith.

MY MOTHER forced me to be a lawyer. I wanted to be a banker. Maybe I was argumentative, logical, tough. There were four of us, all girls, but my mother did not tell my sisters what to do. Her friends tell me she must be laughing up there in heaven, happy about what she made of her eldest child.

I have been a lawyer for 17 years now, but I started to enjoy being one only in 1986. I hated law school, the whole idea of studying again. In England where I lived for 12 years, I never had to attend classes at university. So when I came home for law studies, I found myself fighting the whole American system of education here.

I am still fighting, but in midlife I have learned to choose my battles. I also decide whether something is worth my time and energy or not. If I don't respect you enough, I won't bother with you. If I hate you enough, I'll bother. If I feel the cause is great enough, I'll bother. If I feel it's relevant material or competent, I'll bother. Otherwise, never mind.

There was a time when I would go into everything blindly. Like marriage, law school, leaving England, some relationships I have had, some fights I have had with friends which I should never have bothered with and should have just let go of. At ACCRALAW, every time I wanted to do something drastic, I would consult the senior partners and they would tell me to think it through. I realize now that a lot of my tenacity comes from having worked 18-hour days with them. It was excellent training. I have a hot temper which gets provoked by incompetence, inefficiency and stupidity. It must be because I have set such high standards for myself and I want everyone else to be the same. I guess it's genetic — the Legarda women have always been known to be very strong. And we were always taught that there was nothing we could not do.

My parents separated when my sisters and I were very young, and so we practically never had a male figure. It never occurred to any of us that men are better than us. We plunge into everything with a sense of equality. I guess that's why none of us has been sexually harassed and none of us has had to fight for equal pay— we've always expected it because that was the way we were brought up. It is not fair to make female children think that men are better than they are. That is not how God intended things to be. In fact God made woman out of the rib of man, which shows they are supposed to be equal and one. Adam, in fact, was stupid — he followed what Eve told him.

But I am very shy, even now. I think self-confidence is learned. We were never told that we were good-looking or attractive. We were always told that if we worked hard, we would get what we wanted. There was never any attempt to bring us up feeling conscious about attributes of nature. We had no self-confidence in terms of physical attraction or intelligence, even brilliance. I don't remember ever being told that I was intelligent or good or pretty. We were simply told to work hard if we wanted to get ahead. I realize it wasn't fair to the four of us. My daughter now has more self-confidence than I did when I was her age. Sometimes I tell her she's pretty. I think telling a child that she will really do well if she's pretty and bright and she works hard gives her self-confidence.

I want to tell children not to follow their mothers unless they believe in their minds that their mothers deserve to be emulated because their mothers are strong and work hard and are doing something for themselves other than being with a man. I started my daughter in this frame of mind when she was two years old.

Last year, at a cocktail party, Cardinal Sin told me I should not be advising women to leave their abusive husbands. I said, you know, Cardinal Sin, you are surrounded by 50 nuns who serve you hand and foot, you have no idea how the ordinary family lives in this country. He was stunned. He said maybe I need a little more wisdom. I said I have wisdom, but we have to be practical, you have to see. In fact I have not heard Cardinal Sin say anything in behalf of the child in the Jalosjos case. Nor have I heard any priest tell his congregation not to sell their children. And yet priests tell women not to practise birth control, they should breed children, the children are the future of the Philippines. For sex?

The worst cases I had seen before this child came along were women who put up with battering, emotional abuse, contempt from their husbands because they did not know any better, they thought God would punish them. I don't know why women put up with so much. I don't know if it's because I have lived abroad. I keep telling women, especially young girls who are pregnant and terrified, that it is better to be alone with a child than to be married and lonely. Everyone thinks I'm being ridiculous, or that I'm a man hater. I am neither. There are very few Filipino men who know what the vow of marriage means.

The difference between men brought up here and those brought up abroad is so obvious. I think mothers here are disenabling their sons. Mothers do not teach their sons that there's food on the table because Mommy or Daddy works, that clothes are found clean and pressed in the closet because Mommy and Daddy have organized some maids, or Mommy does it herself. Men leave this kind of home and expect their wives to continue doing these tasks for them. They have no sense of responsibility, of initiative, even of awareness that a home requires certain things. And they certainly have no sense of commitment to a relationship. They see their sisters being brought up to believe that they must never leave their husband, they must serve, be faithful to him. Men are not taught that they are supposed to be faithful, too. And yet women put up with all this. I see them battered and yet they bring up their sons in exactly the same way. When are we going to start saying we will bring up our sons differently?

I am consciously instilling in my two sons the idea of being aware. When they want water they have to go and get it themselves. They're resourceful, they even cook their own meals. They're very sensitive, careful about people's feelings. Since they're very good-looking, I tell them that girls will run after them but they must remember that their mother and their sister are also girls.

WHAT DO I want to do with the rest of my life? Maybe work as a salesgirl in Harrods and meet and marry a rich Arab. But I guess that is not for me. I have no plans, I live from day to day. Every day for me is a new life. I don't even have daily plans. If God told me I would never be able to practise law again and I would have to think of something else to do, I would go into journalism. There's no money in that profession, but there's no money in the kind of law I'm doing now, either. Or maybe I'll get training to be a psychologist and do some counseling. But that would probably drive me crazy, too. Maybe I could teach, but I can't stand teaching stupid people.

I will never marry again. I'm very happy with the way my life has turned out. I've been blessed, I haven't been wanting for my children. I've been able to feed them, send them to school. I want to see them happy and in decent professions, and I'm looking forward to having grandchildren.

Basically, I want to die knowing that I've done the best that I could in my life for everyone I've come across. I want to die with no regrets, so I say yes to everything. If anything should go wrong in the case against Jalosjos, I want to feel that I did my best.

We're all in this world to learn a lesson, otherwise what is the point of our existence? Philosophers have discussed it ad infinitum. I say the purpose of our existence is to learn God's experience in life. I don't go to Mass, but I believe in God. When I wake up in the morning, I say, God, *bahala ka na sa akin* today. And at night before I go to sleep, I say, if I have done anything wrong, please forgive me. That's all it should be. But I have a network of people praying for me, so that I won't be damned for eternity.

Portrait of a Political Activist

NARZALINA Z. LIM

I COME FROM a family of nonconformists. My family tree abounds with characters who are strong-willed and passionate about their beliefs and their loves. My maternal great-grandmother, Petra Gella, was a petite, dark woman with long, black, wavy hair. She and a Spanish *friar* named Fr. Calixto Zaldivar fell in love and had six children. My grandfather, Pedro Telmo Zaldivar, was one of those children.

One of my favorite stories about Lola Petra, which I thought was absolutely romantic, was the fact that she would walk several kilometers for her trysts with the *fraile* in his parish in another town. She would return to her hometown, Pandan, heavy with child. She must have created waves in that small town in the northernmost reaches of Antique. But from all accounts, she was a strong woman who reared her children with dignity.

My mother, her youngest grandchild, is a beautiful blend of East and West. She has dark, soulful eyes, brown skin, sharp features and the patrician bearing of the Castilian priest. Three weeks before I was born in February 1947, my mother lost my father after having been married for only 11 months. Since my mother was only 22 years old, my uncle Calixto Zaldivar took us under his wing. We lived together in one house in Jaro, Iloilo City — my mother, my grandmother and I on the top floor, and my uncle and his family on the ground floor. So even if I was a posthumous child, I grew up with a surrogate father whom I called Papa and enjoyed the warmth and security of an extended family.

My uncle Calixto, named after his Basque grandfather, was a lawyer of note and a dedicated public servant. He had represented our province,

Antique, in the Commonwealth legislature and became governor in the early Fifties. He was my model of an upright and honest government official who, in his long career in government (he was appointed reparations commissioner, then executive secretary to President Diosdado Macapagal in the Sixties before being named to the Supreme Court), never enriched himself nor gave up his principles and beliefs in exchange for money and power. He was a staunch believer in human rights. He taught me to respect the rule of law and to value freedom and democracy. In January 1973, as an associate justice of the Supreme Court, he penned a historic decision. He dissented from his colleagues' opinion recognizing the validity of the 1971 Constitution. He was the only justice to speak out consistently and unequivocally against a sham plebiscite which ratified a constitution clearly crafted to suit the wishes of a dictator. Justice Zaldivar saw the writing on the wall and warned of dire consequences if people did not stand up to Ferdinand Marcos early enough.

In one unforgettable incident, I saw my uncle cry while I was visiting him at his quarters in the Supreme Court. He was crying for our country, he said, because we had lost our civil liberties.

My adopted Papa was one of the respected leaders of the Aglipayan Philippine Independent Church, as my grandfather Pedro Telmo had been in Antique at the turn of the century. It is not clear exactly when or why my grandfather became a staunch follower of Gregorio Aglipay, the rebel Catholic priest who in 1898 joined Gen. Emilio Aguinaldo's revolutionary government against Spain and called on the Filipino clergy to renounce their allegiance to the existing Roman Catholic hierarchy. My grandfather was the son of a Spanish friar so I suppose there was a rebellious streak in him that he inherited from both parents. All I know is that he was an extremely nationalistic man and he brought up his children as nationalists. They all became ardent followers of Aglipay and played leadership roles in their church in Antique.

As a child, I frequented the Philippine Independent Church, where the Philippine flag was prominently displayed by the altar and the national anthem sung at the end of the Mass. My heart swelled with pride every time I imitated my uncle as he put his hand over his breast whenever we sang. Because of the strong nationalism espoused by the Aglipayan Church, I equated love of God with love of country. I did my kindergarten at the Baptist-run Central Philippine University in Jaro, Iloilo, and read Bible stories with American Baptist missionaries who I thought were the kindest people in my young life. We also went to the Catholic Church because my father was Catholic and I was baptized as one.

Occasionally, my Papa would take me with him to the Grand Lodge because he was a 33rd-degree Freemason. I loved being among venerable men dressed in their fancy outfits who talked about incomprehensible subjects. When I read the biography of Jose Rizal, I was thrilled to learn that he, too, had been a Freemason. Although my father's sister was a nun who belonged to the Religious of the Virgin Mary and his brother was a Jesuit, neither of them worried that their young niece was exposed to different religions. My priest uncle always reminded me that the most important thing in life was to allow my mind to soar beyond its normal confines and to have a questioning attitude toward life. I thus grew up in an environment of religious tolerance and had no hang-ups about which God was the true God. I took communion in both Aglipayan and Catholic churches, a practice I still observe today. It helped that I studied in a nonsectarian school, Philippine Women's College, where there were no nuns or priests to condemn me to the fires of hell for socializing with the Masons at the Lodge.

MY PATERNAL heritage is equally colorful. Ancestors from that side emigrated from Fujian Province in China, probably to Pangasinan, from where they set out for other islands, finally to settle in Zamboanga and grow roots there. My great-granduncle, Luis Lim, was the first civil governor of Zamboanga and one of the early journalists of the town. My great-grandfather married a native Subanon and became an adopted chieftain of the community that lived by the *suba* or river. My ancestors, who traded and intermarried with the Malay Muslims, are proof that the immigrant Chinese of the 1700s blended well with the natives of Zamboanga and the neighboring Sulu Sultanate.

I vividly remember childhood summers spent in Zamboanga where bougainvillea grew resplendent everywhere and children dove into the deep for pearls. My paternal grandmother was a member of the big Atilano clan and we had endless family reunions so that I could get acquainted with kith and kin from all over Moroland, for Zamboanga had once been the seat of the so-called Moro Province. Trips to Jolo are best remembered for the crystal clear waters of its beaches and the generosity of my father's sister, *Tita* Tinang, who lived there and was always our gracious hostess. She lives there still, a repository of 93 years of Mindanao history.

I never realized how deeply imprinted those tranquil years were in my memory until I saw Jolo burned to the ground in 1974 during the Marcos regime. As the Christian-Muslim conflict reached its peak and more and more people died, I felt as if a part of me had been killed as well. I never forgave Ferdinand Marcos for the cruelty which his soldiers inflicted on my brother and sister Muslims in that beautiful land.

My other memories of my father's family center on my father's brother, Fr. Hilario Lim, and another uncle, the late senator Roseller Lim, Dad's first cousin. They were two strong personalities who left a mark on me as a young girl. Father Lim was a Jesuit who raised a very important issue relevant to the various religious orders. He pointed out that it was about time Filipino priests were given leadership positions in these orders rather than have foreigners dominate them. He even carried his cause to Congress. I remember him carrying a placard and marching in front of what is now the National Museum building, all by his lonesome self under a blazing sun, to draw attention to his cause. His superiors in the Society of Jesus expelled him from the order on grounds of disobedience and he was banished to the remote areas of the country where he could not cause trouble. He was a brilliant man, an excellent speaker, a scholar and historian. After his expulsion, he always placed an "X J" after his name to remind people and his fellow Jesuits about the cause for which he fought. That lonely crusade of his succeeded in bringing about the Filipinization of the religious orders and in installing the first Filipino president of the Ateneo de Manila, Fr. Francisco Araneta.

When martial law was declared in 1972, Father Lim was arrested and imprisoned in Camp Crame along with many other activists, journalists and politicians who were opposed to Marcos. At the time of his arrest, Father Lim was a history teacher at the University of the Philippines and was at the barricades during the First Quarter Storm of the early Seventies. His circle of friends included Jose Ma. Sison and Nur Misuari, with whom he shared many intellectual pursuits.

My other uncle, Roseller, cut a dashing figure in the Senate during the early Sixties. He was bright and handsome, an orator who once filibustered on the Senate floor for 19 hours nonstop, to delay the election of Ferdinand Marcos as Senate president. *Tito* Ller saw through Marcos and considered him a dangerous person who had to be stopped in his tracks. Alas, Marcos had bought the majority of the senators at that time and did become Senate president, paving the way for his bid for the presidency a few years later. My college classmates and I would sometimes travel all the way from Maryknoll College in Quezon City to the Senate building in Manila just to listen to my uncle debate an issue, for he was a debater par excellence. From him I learned the ways of politics and saw firsthand the workings of the Senate before it became tainted by the machinations of Marcos.

My college years at Maryknoll were happy years. I studied hard during the first two years and made it to the Dean's List. On my third year, I decided that I would not allow my studies to interfere with my education. I exchanged the library for all-night stands with my gangmates in the dorm and a group of La Sallites who became our constant companions. We were notorious in St Joseph's Villa, as the dorm was called, for creeping back early in the morning after dancing all night with the boys and parking in neighboring La Vista subdivision to wait for the sun to rise and the nuns to leave the dorm for morning matins. Those weekend forays were done in the spirit of good, clean fun, and to this day, 30 years later, those boys from La Salle remain our best friends. With them we have bonds too deep and strong to be broken.

I HAVE GONE into this rather lengthy background of my heritage in an effort to understand the roots of my political activism. I myself did not know about such inclinations or about my capacity to rage against oppression until I found myself picketing the grape growers in Delano, California, in July of 1969. I was 22 years old and had just arrived in Santa Barbara to enroll in the Graduate School of the University of California. Foreign students had to undergo a two-month orientation program and our political science professor thought it would be a good idea to expose us firsthand to the issues raised by one Cesar Chavez, leader and organizer of migrant farm workers, mostly of Hispanic origin. Chavez accused the grape growers of exploiting the grape pickers by paying them low wages. On other occasions, he had succeeded in forcing the growers to sign bargaining agreements with his union, the United Farm Workers Organizing Committee.

When we got to Delano, I found many Filipino immigrants among the grape pickers. I interviewed them about their grievances and saw the poor state of their living conditions. My heart went out to my countrymen. Before my professor and our American companions could stop me, I had crossed over to the picket, grabbed a placard and started shouting, "Viva la huelga!" I made it to the front page of the local papers and almost cost the dean of foreign students his job.

In spite of the promise I had to make never again to interfere with the domestic affairs of the United States, I continued to be involved in political activities. In the USA those were the years of student activism provoked by the civil rights movement and the Vietnam War. I could not resist speaking out against the war which I thought the US had no business being in. A few months after the demonstration at Delano, the radicals on campus burned a symbol of the American Establishment, the Bank of America building. Ronald Reagan, then governor of California and president of the regents of the university, had the National Guards sent to our campus to restore peace and order. We had to observe curfew and the university and its surroundings looked like a military zone with uniformed men patrolling every corner. That was my first taste of martial law. It was frightening, considering that the National Guards, during this period, had shot and killed demonstrating students at Kent State University in Ohio.

The University of California was a hotbed of protest. I could not concentrate on my graduate studies and joined instead a moderate political group whose mission was to educate the conservative community in Santa Barbara about the evils of the Vietnam War. I was appalled by the ignorance of the Americans. Many of them did not even know where Vietnam was or why they had to send their boys to fight that war. Our evenings were devoted to house-to-house campaigns and awareness-raising sessions while mornings were devoted to preparing and distributing informative leaflets about US policy in Indo-China.

I learned the skills of mounting street protests and civil disobedience activities at the University of California from 1969 to 1971. It was also during this time that I learned more about the United States and its relationship with the Philippines. I started reading about the US bases in the Philippines and gradually formed an anti-US bases stance. In short, America kindled the latent spirit of political activism within me.

It was at this time that the First Quarter Storm and the Plaza Miranda bombing took place in Manila. My mother sent me clippings regularly to keep me informed of what was happening in the country. I would weep while reading these news reports, thinking that the Philippines was being sundered to pieces and I was not there to help hold it together. I wanted to fly back home and march with the university students who were at the barricades. My mother urged me to see reason and finish what I had gone to the US to do — obtain a master's degree in English literature, which I did. I promised myself, though, that I would go back home as soon as I could, to serve my country in its hour of need.

I came home in April 1972 and proceeded to look for a job. I went to the Senate because I thought that instituting change from within the legal framework of government was the most logical thing to do during those troubled times. I spoke to some senators, for I was no stranger to the Senate, having been exposed to it by my uncle who by then had been appointed justice in the Court of Appeals. I did not like what I saw in the Senate and retreated. Instead I applied for a teaching post at De La Salle University in Taft Avenue where I taught English literature to college students.

Martial law was declared on September 21, 1972, three months after school began. We had to be careful about what we said in class because there were spies all over the place. I became creative and chose to discuss with my class literary pieces which dwelt on the importance of freedom and personal liberties. It was a risk, but I did not see the point of reading literature which did not force my students to assess the precarious condition our country was in.

I took on a full-time job as executive director of Ala-ala Foundation, a private philanthropic foundation owned by the family of Antonio C. Delgado who had set it up to administer scholarships for young people and help alleviate the plight of the poor. Mr. Delgado was a civic leader and the moving spirit behind the formation of the Bishops-Businessmen's Conference (BBC) for Human Development in 1971. Our foundation was very much involved in BBC's activities and nursed the organization from its infancy. I became exposed to priests and nuns who were working in the provinces among the poorest of the poor. During the next five years that I worked for Ala-ala Foundation, I read confidential reports about human rights abuses, arrests without warrants, disappearances of union and peasant leaders, and the strengthening of the Communist Party of the Philippines and its armed group, the New People's Army. Photocopies of these documents began to circulate in Manila. We called the operation "xerox" journalism because the media had been muzzled by Marcos and the only way we could get the news was through the underground press.

The BBC was an excellent forum for discussing what we knew was a very serious political situation. It was an organization of two important pillars of society — church and business — and those of us working on social issues knew that the business community had to be "conscienticized." My close association with this organization served me well when I became a full-time political activist in 1983.

When Ninoy Aquino was assassinated on August 21, 1983, I was ready for the fight against the Marcos dictatorship. My political activism in California and my work with Church-sponsored projects involving the poor and the oppressed had prepared me for the challenges ahead.

On the first night Ninoy's body was brought to Times Street, my friend Ching Escaler and I lined up, along with the crowds, to pay our last respects to the martyr. We were deeply moved by his death and wanted to show our outrage by standing up and being counted among the many who felt the same way we did. We attended the funeral Mass, marched part of the way, and returned home, unable to continue because of the massive crowds. We were not afraid to be identified by Marcos' intelligence apparatus. By killing Ninoy, the Marcos regime gave us the courage to come out in the open and denounce its evils.

After Ninoy had been laid to rest, Ching and I linked up with other women who were just as concerned about the political situation as we were. We started a discussion group and talked about the future of our country, which at that time was on the brink of economic collapse. On September 16, 1983, people in Makati took to the streets in what was the first demonstration ever of the middle forces against the dictator. I remember marching up Ayala Avenue from Buendia, carrying a placard which read "We want justice for Ninoy Aquino!". Winnie Monsod, Tingting Cojuangco, Ching and I marched side by side. It was a sight to see — the middle class, awake at last from its slumber, to demand justice for Ninoy and confront the Marcos regime about its corruption and abuses. Confetti rained down on us from the buildings along Ayala Avenue. That demonstration was a spontaneous combustion of people whose collective frustration and anger found expression in the first of a long series of street protests to demand Marcos' resignation.

We knew that if we wanted to succeed in our mission we had to organize ourselves. Thus, Ching and I formed AWARE, the Alliance of Women for Action Towards Reform. The other founding members of this organization were Winnie, Triccie Sison, Tingting Cojuangco and Guila Maramba. We linked up with the Justice for Aquino, Justice for All (JAJA) Movement, the August Twenty-One Movement or ATOM of Butz Aquino, and the many other organizations which sprouted at this time.

As a full-time political activist, I rarely missed a street demonstration. We were called street parliamentarians then, because we took our issues directly to the people and debated on them in the middle of the street. We formed a tactical alliance with the Left and marched with them to beef up our numbers. It did not matter that they had things on their agenda other than toppling the dictatorship. We found common cause in our desire to drive Marcos out and that served our purpose, temporarily. We ran the risk of being arrested and killed during those demonstrations. For the Marcos regime, the stakes were very high — its continued hold on power. For us, it was the future of our country.

I went into a period of soul-searching. I was a single parent then, with two young children who were only eight and six years old. Their lives depended on me. I dreaded the thought of leaving them orphaned. My maternal instinct told me that my first duty was to look after them and give them the security of my presence. But then again, I reasoned to myself, if I kept away from the struggle, how could I face my children if they should ask, one day, what I did for my country during that dark period of our history? What kind of future faced them anyway, if we did not fight the dictatorship? That future would have been bleak. I did not want my children to live in a country where peace and freedom did not reign. There was no choice but to continue with the struggle.

When Ferdinand Marcos declared the holding of snap elections in late 1985 and Cory Aquino decided to run against him after over a million people drafted her for the presidency, she turned to us women activists to rally behind her and encouraged us to form Cory's Crusaders. She suggested the term "crusader" because she saw the election as a fight between good and evil. The women were to go out on a crusade for good to triumph over evil.

The movement was launched in early December 1985 and the snap elections were slated for February 7, 1986. We had two months to get organized, mobilize nationwide, and get the message of Cory Aquino out to the people. The task of spearheading the movement fell on AWARE. We were ready. The many protest marches and rallies and the networking we had done over the last two years had fully prepared us for this moment. We went to work quickly. Ching was named chairperson of the movement and I was assigned to head the information bureau and to coordinate our activities with the media bureau located on the ground floor of the Cojuangco Building in Makati.

Within five weeks, we organized Cory's Crusaders throughout the country. About 150,000 women signed up voluntarily to assist Cory in her fight against Marcos. They raised money and financed the production of millions of banners, streamers, pins, hats, T-shirts, leaflets and other campaign materials. They educated themselves on the electoral process and listened to experienced people who shared with them information on where and how they thought election fraud might be committed. They trained to become poll watchers for Cory, wore yellow, and were soon dubbed as Cory's "yellow army."

Cory Aquino clearly won that election. The Filipino people made sure that she did, knowing this was the only way they could get rid of the dictator without too much bloodshed. However, as expected, the dark forces of that hated regime stole the people's votes. Massive fraud was committed at the polling places. We saw people clinging to ballot boxes which were being snatched by the Marcos goons in brazen attempts to replace them with boxes stuffed with their own ballots. Many people died defending their votes, defending democracy. While the votes were still being counted, the former governor of Antique, Evelio Javier, was murdered in the capital town of San Jose in broad daylight, in full view of his constituents. Everyone knew that he was killed by hired goons of Arturo Pacificador, the Marcos supporter who was a member of the sham Marcos parliament.

I was one of the first to hear the news about Evelio. I was, as usual, at my post at the media bureau when I received the call informing me of his assassination. Evelio was like a cousin to me. It was my uncle, Justice Zaldivar, who had launched his career in politics by urging him many years before to run for the governorship of our province. Evelio was young and full of dreams, an ideal leader who was able to galvanize the youth in our poor province to change the oppressive structures that kept it under grinding poverty.

All the members of the Zaldivar clan were his loyal supporters. In the 1984 elections for the Batasang Pambansa, two of my cousins and a nephew were massacred by Pacificador's men at a bridge as they were travelling home after campaigning for Evelio. Another cousin was seriously wounded. We had not yet tasted justice for those deaths, nor did we expect to, under Marcos' regime, and now it was Evelio himself who was the victim.

My family was too shocked to move. I was dispatched to Antique immediately to see what I could do and report on the situation there. Fortunately, ABC News had chartered a plane for Antique to cover this hot story there. I hitched a ride and landed in Antique a few hours after Evelio was shot. I saw his body riddled with bullets, lying desolately atop a table in a small room off the town plaza. Nobody had dared to go near it. There was blood all over and the scent of fear hung heavy in the air. The horror and the grief I felt at that moment were equal to the hate I felt for Ferdinand and Imelda Marcos and their minions.

Evelio's assassination was one of the turning points of our struggle. During his wake at Baclaran Church , the ambassadors of some European countries came to express their sympathies and by doing so expressed their governments' support for Cory Aquino as the legitimately elected president of the Philippines. At that point, we knew that international sympathy was with us and it was only a matter of time before support for the Marcos government would be withdrawn.

THIS PART of my life is welded to the history of the Philippines during that tumultuous period just before and during the people power revolution which broke out on February 21, 1986, barely a week after Evelio was buried. I cannot write all the details of that period in this short essay. Suffice it to say that the courage, the strength, and the amazing resiliency and spirituality of the Filipino people triumphed over the forces of evil. Cory Aquino was sworn in as president of the Philippines at a ceremony in Club Filipino which I witnessed at close range. The Marcoses and their supporters fled the country that very day. There was great rejoicing and dancing. All I could think of was to go back to my children whom I had not seen in weeks. I longed to hug them and tell them the whole story of our struggle, one which I had fought for their sake.

But the peace and quiet and the normal life which I sought after three years of marching in the streets were not to be mine. I was still in my yellow T-shirt and rubber shoes when I received a call from Tony Gonzalez, Ninoy Aquino's good friend, with whom I had worked closely during the campaign for Cory. He said that President Aquino had just appointed him minister of tourism, would I please help him run the ministry?

I thought he was joking. I could not see myself running a government ministry. But Tony was dead serious. He insisted that I join him when he went to the Ministry of Tourism to "take over" from Jose Aspiras, Marcos' first minister of tourism who had served in that capacity for over a decade. I refused. I said I was tired and wanted to be left alone with my children whom I had neglected for many years. Besides, I said, I did not like the Ministry of Tourism. I used to march with my women friends past that building on T.M. Kalaw Street and Rizal Park to protest the organized sex tourism which flourished in the late Seventies and early Eighties, which was clearly condoned, if not encouraged, by the ministry. That ministry, I said, was used by the Marcoses to window-dress the stench and corruption of their regime and I had no respect for it. What irony that I would even be considered to serve there!

Tony was insistent and so was I. It was a tug-of-war. I cried for many days, refusing to accept the fact that I was being called to serve my country once again and yet knowing, deep inside me, that it was my duty to respond to the call to help rebuild from the ruins left by the Marcos regime. I recalled President Aquino talking to us women volunteers shortly after the snap elections. She said that if we succeeded in our cause and she won, we had to continue to help her run the country because she was not prepared to be president and we all had to be in there together. At that time I did not pay much attention to Cory's words because all I could think of was whether we would come out of that struggle alive. I was resigned to die for my country and did not entertain any thought of what we would do, if indeed, by some miracle, we would come out victorious.

Well, the miracle had happened and a decision was staring me in the face. With a heavy heart and full of trepidation, I reported to the Ministry of Tourism on March 1, 1986. On March 15, I was sworn in as deputy minister, and a few days later, I attended my first Cabinet meeting, my boss having gone to Malaysia to spread the news to the world, through an international tourism conference, that the Philippines was back in business. After that Cabinet meeting, President Aquino announced that she was opening up Malacañang Palace to the people. The Filipino people, she said, had been shut out of that Palace for so long and now she wanted it to be the people's

Palace. She also wanted the people to see for themselves how the Marcoses had lived and to understand from their excessive lifestyle why the people turned against them. The President wanted the MOT to handle the tours of Malacañang.

That announcement opened the floodgates. Hundreds of thousands of people trooped to the Palace demanding to get in. Those who could not enter went to the MOT, asking for tickets for the tour. I recall thousands of people crowding Rizal Park in front of our building, impatiently waiting for word from us about when they could take their tour. It was like people power in EDSA all over again. Fortunately, my years as a street parliamentarian had trained me to handle big crowds and to use a megaphone effectively. We eventually pacified the highly emotional crowd and promised that everyone would have a chance to see Malacañang and Imelda's shoes.

My fellow women marchers volunteered to help get the Palace ready for the tours and to put a system in place so that these could be conducted in an orderly fashion. Guides had to be trained quickly. The spirit of volunteerism, the euphoria generated by the success of people power at EDSA, the elevated feeling of being liberated from the bondage of dictatorship helped us accomplish the formidable task of opening up Malacañang to the public at such short notice. Aside from President Corazon Aquino, the housewife who fought the dictator, Malacañang Palace became the biggest tourist attraction in the mid-Eighties.

Our tourism program had to be refocused. I was of the firm belief that a sound tourism program should have domestic tourism as its base. A country whose people know, appreciate and love their own country will promote itself. The Filipino people did not have the inclination or the money to travel around their own country during the martial law years. Their own Ministry of Tourism emphasized international tourism. It bragged about having attracted a million international tourists in 1980, never mind that half of these were Japanese men who came for sex. Only the numbers mattered. The MOT claimed that the Marcoses were doing something good for the country, that's why tourists came in droves.

Our task was to change the image of the Philippines from a sex tour destination to a wholesome destination. The country was billed as the "Fiesta Islands." The rich culture and heritage and the courage of the Filipino people in standing up to a dictator were the magnets used to draw visitors back into the country. We stood proud and tall in the eyes of the world. It worked, but the bubble burst quickly. The new government was racked by coup attempts and dissension among its appointed officials. When the new Constitution had been framed and ratified in 1987, elections for Congress and other elective positions were held. Faces of old traditional politicians resurfaced and the whole political arena looked like a revival of the Marcos era. Those of us who had marched in the streets became disillusioned. We did not have the stomach for the dirty politics of old and the corruption which we saw creeping back into the system. We were too idealistic. It did not take us very long to realize that it was easier to kick out a dictator than to hold a newly restored democracy together in one whole piece. The spirit of people power began to evaporate as people with whom we had walked the streets went their separate ways and those who had joined government in 1986 began to leave.

JOINING the government was a traumatic experience for me. I was more comfortable in my yellow T-shirt, organizing street protests, than I was in the corridors of power where the air was heavy with intrigue and political maneuvering. To this day, I look upon my years in government as unhappy years. The government was weak and unstable. It had to fend off one coup attempt after the other. There were several Cabinet revamps, reflecting the instability of the administration. I served three secretaries of tourism and held the Department of Tourism (DOT) together, providing it the continuity it needed during those years of change. I lasted the full term of President Aquino, one of the few of her original appointees who managed to serve for six full years. Toward the end of her term, she appointed me secretary of tourism. I had just completed a very important assignment then, which early on I decided would to be my legacy to the tourism industry. This was the 20-year Tourism Masterplan of the Philippines, which I worked on for a year with a team of international and local consultants and my staff at the department. It was with a great sense of accomplishment that I presented that to President Aquino because it was something I had worked hard on and I believed it was a tangible contribution to her government's tourism program.

When Fidel V. Ramos succeeded Mrs. Aquino as president in June 1992, he reappointed me and I served in his Cabinet for a short period. Then I asked him to let me go. I said I had packed my bags as early as May when Mrs. Aquino's transition team was working on the orderly transfer of her government to his. I was honored to have been part of that orderly transition and my job was done. President Ramos understood, and in October 1992 I finally returned to the private sector where I knew I belonged.

Postscript: A book about women of passion would not be complete if it did not include affairs of the heart in it. My love affairs, I hope, will one day be written by my daughter, who is now 19 and has shown great sensitivity, intellectual maturity and a keen interest in the literary craft. She can probably interpret a life lived unconventionally, for I bore her and her brother outside the confines of marriage and brought them up single-handedly while I lived out history from the Seventies to the Nineties. I did not believe then that marital commitment would work for me, considering my rebellious and headstrong nature, my strong sense of independence, and my commitment to political causes and eventually to public service. I changed my mind in 1991 when I met Ludwig Rieder, who was sent to the Philippines to be the chief technical adviser for the Philippine Tourism Masterplan Project which I had initiated at the DOT and was funded by the United Nations Development Programme and the World Tourism Organization. To me, he was heaven-sent. After all the joys and pains of past loves, I finally saw in him a person with whom I could commit a lifetime. We were married by Fr. Joaquin Bernas, S. J., in 1992 with my children, our immediate families and only our closest friends in attendance. It was a beautiful wedding, as weddings should be, full of gaiety and the warmth of true friendships. I was 45 years old and a new chapter of my life had just begun.

Surprised by Joy

Julie Lluch

MY GREAT-GRANDMOTHER lived a few months short of a hundred years; her son, my grandfather, close to 98 years. My father is robust at 84 and still drives his car around Metro Manila like a seasoned taxi driver. Granting that I, following in the footsteps of my family's famous tenacity for life and surviving the poisons of the environment, live to be 80 or 90, I should now be past the middle of my life. Optimistically, I can expect to live 10, 20 or 30 more years of earthly existence, but I also know that I could just as well go tomorrow, today or next year. Not really too morbid a thought for one who is older and more accustomed to the thought of death and dying. But then, wisely, I have begun to number my days.

* * *

I could have just chosen to dismiss it as a nonevent, but that would be dodging. At 50 and awaiting its visitation or non-visitation, I will be damned writing about the climacteric — that cumbersome figure lurking at the corner, mysterious and life-threatening, around it a company of sinister myths and neuroses of every streak and strain.

Approaching the end of the reproductive years is a difficult time, admittedly. It may be that I've read too much feminist and existentialist literature, or the wrong kind, but the menopausal syndrome is said to be particularly severe on intelligent women who like to investigate.

As a heartrendingly naive feminist in the early Eighties, I mourned the "death of the womb" as women's ultimate defeat and raised a fist to heaven for such cosmological injustice. Jealous and bitter, I wrote in an essay:

Sometimes I wonder if my involvement with the women's movement has enlarged or constricted my consciousness, if it has made me sympathetic or intolerant of humanity, with other women especially. Has my world vision become distorted? I have begun to suspect that the so-called natural order of things isn't so natural at all. Commonplace things appear questionable: Is woman's place really in the home? Is woman's position in coitus naturally supine? Even as I uphold the principle of authenticity of individual experience, I question the righteousness of my rage. God forgive me if this towering emotion is no more than envy, the feminist perspective being what it is — seeing and feeling the relative deprivation of power or favor and painfully discovering the overwhelming fact that society serves its men better than its women. Cain would have been Woman! Abel was better loved by God!

* * *

To openly confront the issue of the climacteric is to render oneself vulnerable, virtually to concede defeat and admit to one's inadequacies, loneliness and fears. Better to shut up and let the storm pass. But it is to the credit of the feminists to have shed light on this controversial aspect of woman's experience. It is in facing up squarely to the fact of the climacteric that a woman uncovers and destroys the hidden male constructs which have crippled her psychologically. The loss of youth is an issue intimately related to the climacteric and the feminist points out that a woman should not wait till midlife before she fights to overthrow the standards and dirty devices of a world that would demand of her to be pleasing, beautiful, sexually potent and young forever.

In midlife, a woman comes to terms with her biological destiny. The feminist's quarrel is not with God who makes all things good (who wants babies at 50?). Her quarrel is with the powers that be in a world that oppresses and corrupts.

* * *

From the movement I learned a basic tenet: woman's freedom is something she earns and claims for herself. It is she who enters the cleansing fires and she herself who must define her experience. Emerging from the trying climacteric years, the older woman should have acquired serenity and power that allows freedom and a higher kind of love. The wiser, older woman should have left behind the clamorous life of jealousy, insecurity and the trappings of romantic love, and go on to embrace the warmth, depth and riches of selfless, uncorrupted love.

One of the earliest sculptural busts I did as a young artist was that of Jose Garcia Villa whom I had never met. I made him out like a unicorn, mystical and erotic, an arrogant protuberance of a horn grown out of the middle of his forehead. It was my humble tribute to this intriguing poetic genius. At that point in time, my life was such that I simply could not have enough of it and no poet so eloquently expressed my predicament as Villa did when he wrote:

> Always did I seek more god
> than life could yield,
> more god than God could give.

I'm not sure which big letter went with which god but when I tried switching and substituting the key words, the meaning, at least for me, didn't really change much:

> Always did I seek more life (art)
> than God (life) could give
> more life (art) than life (art) could yield.

Art was the overarching passion when Christianity overtook me in midlife with its quiet invasion of transfiguring grace. The artistic life was the context encompassing a homespun feminism and a perilously uncontexted sexuality against which the authentic life of Christ was reborn in me. The Lord God of Christianity would show me that all of man's desiring begins and ends in Him alone. I was drawn to this passionate God who spared nothing but gave His own life for love of man and demanded, nay, commanded that we love Him in return with all our heart, soul, mind and strength.

As an artist, what I found initially irresistible about Christianity was this all-consuming fire, a love as strong as death. In a time of brokenness when human love all but failed and all around the valley looked dark and deep, I succumbed to the sweet invitation of absolute forgiveness and an unconditional love that led straight to the Wedding Feast.

> "Arise, my love, my fair one, and come away with me,"
> the lover calls to his beloved bride in the Song of Songs.

Rightly or wrongly, an artist is commonly perceived as a creature cursed or blessed with intense responses to the things around him. I guess

I conformed to that pat image scandalously to a T. In youth, one was supposed to breathe art, eat and defecate art, make one's person the living manifesto of the inseparable unity of Art and Life. I carried the identification quite far, to the point of artlessness, and literally "became" my artwork. I could point to any one of my self-portraits in my narrative sculptural tableaus and say, "That sculptured woman cutting onions is me, and I am she. What makes us different is that she is clay and I am flesh. But we're both real and the stories that we tell are the same."

* * *

I worried that becoming Christian would mean the end of creativity. I would lose the pagan instincts that fire the imagination and primitive urges to heights of creative power in art, poetry and music. My work would become stale, washed-out and dead, as if the very life-blood was suctioned out of my system. Christianity, I decided, was the exact antithesis to the life of the senses, and I resigned myself to what Thoreau describes as a life of quiet mediocrity.

But in relenting to the stark gospel of the Cross, I was suprised by the joyful relief of divine humor and knew the absolute futility of the devil's lies. My art didn't perish, I only stopped being a "mere" artist. To be converted to faith is to step into a realm of paradoxes and take on an even more relentless engagement with life, too intense even for art, but knowing a peace that "passes human understanding."

I read that becoming spiritual is just a phase in the natural human life cycle, a predictable step midlifers commonly make on the way to senility: saying goodbye unself-pityingly to one's youth and shifting perspective from the here-and-now to God's eternity. Maybe so, maybe not, depending on one's understanding of what spirituality really means, because I actually know more youths than older men and women who walk in the Spirit-life.

Feminists and psychologists agree that midlife is the time most conducive to spirituality for various practical and obvious reasons. I believe the coming to end of the millennial age has much to do with the global upsurge of interest in matters spiritual. Of late we have been hearing of studies and researches being conducted on the subject and meditation and dream analysis and other like activities being practised among NGOs and women's groups — a development that as a feminist I wholeheartedly endorse. But then again, I have ceased to be a mere feminist.

* * *

Not that I have any right to ask or know, but I have wondered if in life Villa found the God for whom he thirsted so in his poetry. Does it matter if he did, or does his poetry alone suffice? Perhaps in seeking God so intensely, and when the heart is right, the seeker has already found Him?

* * *

The pursuit of art, if not revitalized by positive faith, may be just so much "decayed refinement" or "refined decay," as one poet puts it. It can lead the artist to worship the Baals of the Intellect, in the temples of Earth and Eros — the generative forces of the universe that fertilize and feed man's creative impulses naturally depraved from their Adamic origins. Art is a most powerful impulse, and very dangerous, too, because it comes closest to divinity. I have no doubt Lucifer was an artist before he became a rebel. In fact the Bible says he was a musician, a beautiful archangel who led the heavenly choir in singing worship to Almighty God. How often, while listening to Beethoven's Ninth Symphony, I get a spirit-lift and cry, "Paradisiacal!" or catch myself muttering at Picasso's Bullfight series, "Diabolical!"

No, I don't mean Picasso is damned. It's just my way of saying how stunned I am by the sheer size of his artistic gift. For all his excesses, Picasso was a true servant of art. I imagine him dying a thousand times for his work and that must have called for a lot of faith.

* * *

It may sound like silly child's play but I do care if my beloved artists make it or have made it to the real Paradise — you know, Milton's and Dante's? Talk about idle spiritual gossip, but I have no doubt about Bach, Beethoven and Handel, Milton, Michelangelo, Dostoevsky, etcetera. Yes! They who have given us through their works a foretaste of heaven and made life bearable on this groaning planet.

After watching Goethe's play, *Faust*, a couple of years ago, I asked a friend in earnest if she believed that Faust, who sold his soul to the devil but cried to Christ for help in the end, was saved. She, of course, just looked at me with a quizzical eyebrow. I knew it was only a play, and what did it matter if Dr. Faustus burned in hell since he was only a fictional protagonist anyway. But it was important for me to know and I couldn't explain why.

* * *

I grew up in a house that music filled all day long. In the evening after family supper, when everyone had retired to the bedrooms, Papa would often relax in the living room, comfortable in his loose robe over pajamas, his all-too-familiar French beret protecting his head from the draft. He would pick out an LP to play on the old phonograph, dim the lights, sit on his favorite sofa, lean back, close his eyes, and listen. The eager copycat that I was, I snuggled up beside him, leaned back, closed my eyes, and unsuspectingly launched on my lifelong adventure with the classics. Even for just the memory of that one uneventful night with my father, I will thank and love him beyond a lifetime.

* * *

I have few memories of childhood, a good indication that it was a happy one. Indeed I must have been the happiest little girl on earth for as long as I was singing and dancing, which I did with lusty fervor. (I thought then, as I do now, that "Silent Night, Holy Night" was the most beautiful song of all.) But at the age of eight or nine, I stopped singing.

Across the street from my father's house lived a billboard painter. He was the first painter I'd known and I think he was a good one, too. But he was drunk most of the time, cursed, threw things around the house, and sometimes beat up his children. His wife, a seamstress, was a kind and gentle woman who bore him 12 children, including a set of twins. So I'd come to play with the children or I'd come to watch, with intent fascination, the painter while he painted, even if he reeked with alcohol. And because I was an obedient child I sang when he asked me and he was very pleased. But when he got too drunk he made me promise to sing for him when he is dead. "You will sing for me, child, or my ghost will come for you at night and drag you off your bed," he spoke with grave and cruel humor. Not long after, the man died, stabbed several times by a crazed drunk right there in our neighborhood.

I saw and heard of that long, hot afternoon more things than my tender memory could hold for a long time afterward. The knife glinted in the sun as the murderer raised his bloody hands and faced the shocked crowd that had gathered. He smiled, took a deep, elegant bow, as at a performance's end, and slowly, theatrically, laid down the weapon on the ground. The police grabbed him. I saw the lifeless body of the painter carried to the police jeep and whisked away. Then I remembered my promise.

Holding back tears, I sang Schubert's *Ave Maria* at his funeral, my voice and frail body trembling in fear and buried anger because death's face was ugly and shattered my joyful little world.

The discovery of clay as my personal medium was a turning point in my artistic career. My "inordinate" attachment to it can only be described as idolatrous, in the secular sense, that is. I was bound to it with a bond so strong that our two natures seemed to blend mystically and flow as one. I have written paeans to this wondrous earth matter which to this day has remained as elusive and mysterious as it was for me in the beginning.

I share excepts from an article, "Notes from a Potter's Life," I wrote in the late Seventies, early in my dalliance with the medium.

I love to think of clay as the most apt poetic metaphor for artistic creation. It is a very sensuous medium — soft, obedient and pleasurable to the touch. The artist is in most immediate contact with it, working directly with hands and body.

I derive almost childlike delight working in this medium, remembering the time in childhood when playing with dirt and mud was such grievous misdeed. Clay is a natural plaything and touching it revives old instincts. The thing is to let them out as fast as I can, spontaneously and joyously.

* * *

I liken the potter to the primitive brujos of Carlos Castañeda's landscape whose secret knowledge of nature is the source of their powers. The potmaker of old is an accomplice of nature. In making a pot, he waits for the right season, the correct time of day, chooses the exact spot on the earth, the elevation, aridity, humidity. He checks the turn of the wind, the color of fire, and after attending to a hundred and one preparations, waits and prays for the unseen powers to favor the work of his alchemy.

* * *

I see the potter meditatively bent over the turning wheel, out of which rises a vessel of clay. That, I tell myself, is how I shall spend the days of my old age, turning out magical pots in some quiet retreat near the mountain or beside the sea.

* * *

Like Mary after her fiat at the Annunciation, every artist is a birthgiver, called to serve his work every moment of its birthing. He listens to it, obeys it in all humility and truth, knowing that in the end the work is greater than himself. Madeleine L'Engle, a Christian writer of children's books, writes of art as an "incarnational activity" and the artist at work as being "in a condition of complete and total faith."

* * *

Looking through my work as in a retrospective, I am at once amazed and chastised at what it has to teach me about myself. The later period particularly reads like an allegory of one person's unregenerate search for meaning. Whereas the early nudes, landscapes, portraits of friends, poets, artists and family members were innocuous affirmations of life, and whereas the middle works of eroticized cacti and hearts playfully celebrated love and sexuality, the later works were disturbing expressions of a disturbed psyche. Consciously or unconsciously, in these narrative tableaus of women in a domestic locus or in other situations, I projected my increasing anxieties and fears. Ultimately, my fear of death and annihilation.

* * *

Above everything else, the artist wants life. All his strivings are simply to assure himself that he is alive. But the paradox is this: the more he would cling to life, the more death becomes an imminent reality. This could be partly what Jesus meant when he said, "Anyone who would save his life would lose it, and he who would lose his life for the sake of God, would save it."

* * *

After giving birth to my third daughter, I hovered on the brink of a breakdown. The doctors put me heavily on depressants and I walked around the house like a zombie unable to care for my baby. As many times as I was rushed to emergency because I was dying, so many times the nurses told me it was all in my mind which was going, going. Fiercely, I held on to the last weak strands that held together my sundered selves. I didn't know Jesus then, but he was there surely, through it all. And so it was during this dark night of my life when I hit upon this wild idea that I could somehow save myself — through art.

I dropped everything — the psychiatric and hypnotic sessions and trances and my floundering teaching job at a girls' convent school — and announced to my surprised husband that I was going to be what I really wanted to be — an artist! The idea wasn't really that wild because I had always known even as a child that unless I was being a creator, I wasn't fully alive.

* * *

A fulfilled sculptor reeling from a failed marriage many years later, I created *"Sunog!"* ("House on Fire!", terra cotta, 1991). In this sculpture piece a woman is frantically screaming for help from her house which is burning. Everyone else in the house sleeps peacefully — the cat, dog, rooster, cow and the naked woman. All except two geckos mating. A sense of impending devastation pervades these later works. In "Piscean Deluge" (terra cotta and acrylic, 1990) a naked woman swims for dear life as she is buffeted by powerful wind and waves. She is sinking with the farm animals — the cow, the horse and the chickens — into the watery depths. Wherever she was — in a dream, as a symbol, in the desert, or in flood and fire — the woman at the center of the clay works is pathetically perishing.

Sapped of strength, defeated and tired, I laid her to rest finally. The clay woman had to die. With typical abandon of one newly found in the faith, I created "Doxology" in 1993. This life-size work consists of two figures representing the two selves of the same woman. One lies sprawled on the floor, cold and lifeless. The other stands resplendently alive, her arms outstretched in worship and her gaze fixed longingly upon heaven.

Madeleine L'Engle again speaks: "Nothing is created without this terrible entering into death. It takes great faith, faith in the work, if not faith in God, for dying is fearful. And if we die willingly, no matter how frightened we may be, we will be found, and born anew into life, and life more abundant."

* * *

Toward finishing the shooting for her award-winning short film, *"Asong Simbahan,"* my daughter Issa felt she still lacked something, perhaps a powerful visual to pull the film through. She was listless. Just a few months ago, she had shot the same entire scenes and episodes in the very same locations in that quaint town beside Laguna Lake. A technical malfunctioning in processing damaged the negatives and she had to reshoot 90 percent of the episodes. Emotionally and financially, it had been disastrous.

The sun was going down, promising a glorious sunset at the lake on this last afternoon of shooting. Issa now knew what she needed but had to hurry off everyone, cast and crew, to the lake before the light died out. The film, which crams more dogs in one church scene than in any movie you've seen, is about a painter's young daughter who puts her faith in the Lord. To render this spiritual event in cinematic terms, director Issa wanted to shoot the girl, who is played by younger sister Krista, walking on water! Seeing a long wooden bench in the house (waiting there for the fulfillment of its hour of destiny), Issa seized it and had it brought to the lake. At the shallow part of the lake was a concrete slab on which fishermen haul in their day's catch. Issa placed the wooden bench on top of this concrete flooring which was now underwater because the tide had come in. It could only have been by God's perfect design that the height of the bench was just so that the water barely covered it. An hour or half an hour late or early, the water level would not have been the same.

The cameras roll. Krista prays on a fisherman's boat in the middle of the lake. Behind her the sea and sky meet breathtakingly. Slowly, she rises, steadies herself, then steps out of the boat. The camera cuts to medium shot as her foot rests on the unseen wooden plank. Step by careful step she moves over the submerged bench, the soles of her feet barely skimming the surface of the lake. The camera pulls back. The young girl stretches out her arms in front of her. The music rises. The wind stirs. She walks on the water — onto the arms of her waiting God.

From the Calendar of Anger
A poem in progress
BABETH LOLARGA

. . . I rise
every morning like a waning
moon on a new world I
do not care for but mean
to survive whole to change.

—Marge Piercy

1.

when my malignant womb declared
it was time for it to go,
for a month a rosy rivulet
passed out of me,
soaking maxi pads
with what i imagined,
with what i wanted to be
just mulberry or wild strawberry
stains. a colleague worried
that i might be miscarrying,
i who had stupidly aired
a faint desire for a third offspring.

& i thought,
like mary before the angel,

how can that be
since i know not
man (nor for that matter
Holy Rapist Ghost)?

2.

the marriage bed had long grown
unfamiliar to my slowly thickening body,
the mattress tilting towards
one abandoned occupant's side.
to my girlhood home & single bed
with my second child
i fled, my second try
at leaving overrated
supposedly happilyeverafterland.

actually it was an inaccessible cottage
on a suburban hill
where the men kept game cocks
while faded women sweetened homegrown yams
& wrapped sticky rice with banana leaves.

there my children's father,
showing a side foreign to me,
puttered, potted & pruned,
weeded & tirelessly tidied,
planted a fire tree & mahogany
to mark a first child's birth.
displaced were dwarfs who played
evil mischief, raising unexplainably
high fevers in a maid's son,
swelling his cheeks
like a frog in chorus,
then pressing scales on
my baby's sweet soft scalp.

3.

i used to slap a square of ham,
whatever piece of fried cured meat,
the contents of a tiny tin of liver spread

on slices of buttered white bread,
the quick-fix sandwich
for my man on the go,
the adrenaline addict
who would drop me,
the inconvenient, inconsequential baggage,
in the midst of stalled traffic
or on a flooded junction

while he rushed off
to his world of utter import,
a meeting, a briefing, a consulting
of similar unfeeling pros.

4.
but this i must say,
i must insist go on the record
when all the petty vileness
has been expended:

always, despite the unsatisfactory-
because-obligatory sex, he was concerned
that i come,
that somehow his fifty, sixty,
possibly even seventy
earnest thrusts were not for naught.
roll over he did not,
not until he felt the start
of a shudder, a slight
wind on his cheek,
the folds of my cunning cunt
& moist muscles
squeezing the tip of his dick,
his fluids finally home in my sea.

then all exertions evaporated —
no cozy, post-coital nuzzling whatsoever,
no reaching for comforting, leftover warmth,
not the dimmest prospect
of a soulful sharing of intimacies.

better yet to masturbate,
my teacher told me once,
than have the common others say
your brain has dripped down on
your husband's hardly superb performing
loins.

5.

individual beds &,
whenever possible, separate quarters,
my family of four concluded,
assured less frictions,
honored private space,
allowed a greater tolerance for
personal mess. but still
he bested me
(not that i really cared)
in scrub-all, clean-up weaponry
that supported his lifestyle
of sanitary, well-screened,
conspicuous sanity.

Up & Over the Convent Wall

SYLVIA L. MAYUGA

FIVE DECADES since my father charmed his way past Japanese sentries to get my mother to a hospital in time for me, I have come to believe that every soul chooses the circumstances of its birth. This idea tossed from roiling depths of human consciousness up the high spiritual surf of the Sixties and Seventies instantly struck me as a more satisfying version of an early catechism lesson: that one is born "to know, love and serve God and be happy with Him forever in heaven."

Today I belong to a tribe that has long stopped referring to God as a "Him." Though by definition beyond either-ors, a Creator who allows human souls the choice of their historical time and place, parents and environment sounds more female than male to me. Such a Being, I believe, must be too busy prodding human children to new fields of beauty, surprise and adventure to spend much time on a throne surrounded by adoration while passing stern patriarchal judgment on cowering human souls.

A serious downside is what I understand to be another rule of incarnation: that with its first earthly breath, the soul forgets the life-script it has coauthored and must sometimes spend entire lifetimes trying to remember. This, it is said, is due to the difference in the nature of matter and spirit — the origin of that subtle emotion called nostalgia whose original meaning is "a longing for one's origin in the stars."

My earliest experience of nostalgia could have been a childhood discovery that I could not extend frequent flying dreams to my waking hours. This may explain the speed with which I gravitated to ballet and a prospect of someday hurtling clear across a stage to music. Alas, an early heart murmur forced me to give that up, too. Tearful every time a symphony overture began and curtains opened on a stageful of ethereal ballerinas that did not include me, I grudgingly slid down the ladder of material reality to slowly sublimate into a writer thirsty for levitation.

It goes without saying that I have also reexamined and come to redefine the Christ somewhat differently from convent school: as a template for human souls so perfect it can coax music even from all the embarrassing noise I've made breaking molds in a struggle to be free. Enough scars attest to my efforts at clambering up the high stone walls that surrounded Catholic convent-bred Filipinas in the Fifties. Traumas major and minor attended my sprint past the gates of conventional wisdom to young adulthood. There the outlines of my forgotten life-script glimmered in the smoke of Molotov cocktails and psychedelics. But that is getting ahead of the story.

A major benchmark emerged when I was a fifteen-year-old high school senior chosen to represent St. Scholastica's College in an oratorical contest called Voice of Democracy in the late Fifties. This led me straight to the tectonic faultline of my era. Not only had I been recruited into an ideological army on the march against a Communist bloc ruled by mythical monsters like those that had once inhabited the edges of a Flat Earth.

The VOD also brought me into unequal contest with the fearsome Guardian of the Gate. It began innocently enough in an affectionate personal letter I wrote St. Benedict for a schoolwide essay contest on SSC's Golden Jubilee. The first prize it won may have given school authorities the impression that I was also a natural advocate for the Free World. They had not counted on the nascent free-thinking that came with my early delight in the Word.

Given free rein to write my speech, I counted democracy's blessings in freedom of thought, speech and worship. I was summoned to Mother Superior's office soon after its submission. Pale skin matched by crisp white habit, the August One came straight to the point. Freedom of thought and speech were fine but I had gone too far with "freedom of worship." As a good Catholic girl, I should know that there is "no salvation outside the Church." I was therefore to delete that last freedom from my speech.

I don't remember saying very much in my terrorized state but do recall my first reaction: there goes the rhythm of my sentence. Tummy doing a loop-the-loop as I raced back to the classroom, the next dark thought was that Mother Superior had just consigned all non-Catholics to hell. My youthful horizons had yet to include live Muslims, Jews, Hindus, Buddhists, Parsees, Sikhs and Shintoists. Yet something inside me kicked violently against the August One's edict. "She has no right!" a fifteen-year-old convent girl thought, trembling.

The offending phrase stayed in a speech that won second prize. But there was hell to pay back in SSC. Not only did Mother Superior refuse to accept my trophy. Her long fingers reached into my report card where a low grade in Conduct quickly disqualified me from delivering the valedictory speech at graduation. My parents' disappointment at their eldest daughter's fate tasted like dust and ashes. But the story had just begun. The price for my first heresy would turn out to be a tuition fee to more expansive worlds.

First there were other serious barriers to leap over. Fearing that my rebellious spirit, now unmasked, would instantly turn me into an agnostic and/or a Communist if I were let loose in a nonsectarian State University in early free-thinking ferment, my father decreed enrollment in a second convent school for college. My life-script was unfolding.

Still licking the wounds of my first unsuccessful struggle for self-determination, I found myself amid a gaggle of young women all with their own honors from schools all over the country. Later we would be told that St. Theresa's College's A.B. '63 was a rare collection. That we had converged at the beginning of an exciting transition for Christendom and, it turned out, the history of human consciousness itself, seemed part of the script.

Members of the last Filipino generation to learn the Catholic Mass in Latin, we would live to see priests make a 360-degree turn on the altar to face and include us more intimately in the celebration. Wonder of wonders, this Mass would also be translated from sonorous Latin to melodious Tagalog — the native tongue whose depth and humor escaped us for years after our systematic alienation from it by years of demerits for saying "Why *naman*?" on campus. In this sidewise fashion did genteel neo-colonialism begin to teach us all forms of rebellion.

Later they would add up to nervous breakdowns and a high rate of failed marriages paradoxically paired with a roster of worldly achievements hitherto unthinkable for Filipinas. Back then, ritual Saturdays that began with early morning Mass in a spotless chapel with a smooth marble floor and a tinkling golden bell topped the list of what I loved most about convent school. In a state of exaltation, my fellow Sodalists and I next swooped into squatter shanties growing like fungi under the neighboring Ayala Bridge. Bearing US Aid flour and secondhand clothes, we taught catechism and awkwardly tried to "validate" live-in arrangements between spectral beings twice our age in the name of "propagating the Faith."

The speed with which we next changed from blue and white uniforms to "outside dress" to head for the movies and bookstores indicated that the innocent arrogance of our early forays into urban poor country did not go very deeply into our psyches. Little did we know that those ritual Saturdays were a virtual training camp for translating, one to the other, the many contradictory worlds coexisting in the Philippines.

For hours on end, my *barkada* and I then fell to comparing notes on the words and exploits of our favorite teachers — Sisters Jose and Ignatia, two irreverent originals who first taught us psychology, philosophy and literature. The bits and pieces of learning they offered became bright strands in the provisional worldview our covey of schoolgirls wove together on those long Saturday afternoons. For knots, we exchanged an unending stream of poetic and philosophical quotations casting light on the conundrums of teenaged female lives blossoming in a hermetic milieu.

Products of more progressive schools would later josh me for all the years of schooling I spent in uniform. I would hear none of it. If SSC led to a discovery of my stubborn independent streak, STC fortified me in an introspective, creative sisterhood, a kind of female mafia attached to a larger network of young people who would not be kept from peering under the unswept rugs of the One True Church for long.

The good nuns needn't have bothered to tailor-make our reading lists with a bias for "safe" Catholic authors. They only gave edge to our constant search for unlocked bolts in and around the gates of eternal salvation. Quietly we challenged everything from a gut feeling that our lives depended on the quality of disturbing questions shared with our peers.

The La Sallites were great dancers but it was the Ateneans who clued us to look beyond St. Augustine to modern theologians like Niebuhr, Tillich and Buber for deeper lights on our received Christianity. From our UP friends came our first inkling of the political turbulence soon to burst outside our convent walls. On this trail came our discovery of unsanctioned thinkers like the existentialist philosopher Jean Paul Sartre who exercised our minds but left our hearts cold and the controversial psychiatrist Sigmund Freud who aroused our sympathy for his tedious labors over the sexual mores of the Victorian era.

But the arrows that hit bull's-eye belonged to our two fellow *colegialas* half a world away, the Frenchwoman Simone de Beauvoir and the American Mary McCarthy. *Memoirs of a Catholic Girlhood* and *The Second Sex* brought gasps of self-recognition in our common experience of contradiction between "convent school" and "education."

A climax to independent discovery came soon after senior year, from a book entitled *The Phenomenon of Man* by the French Jesuit Teilhard de Chardin. Nothing in my experience could have prepared me for that life-changing encounter with a fascinating combination of scientist, priest and seer. His study of paleontology confirmed spiritual intuitions that, to my wonderment, also whispered to a chit of a girl trying to make sense of a huge starry universe with skimpy input.

In essence, he said that life on earth was all about travelling an upward spiral to full consciousness where, at the climax called "Omega Point," humanity would come to know and rejoice in itself as a single organism with one heart and mind. All beings had been created for this grand enterprise, its completion awaited with longing by the Creator.

I had met my first cosmic Catholic thinker, more interested in divining God's design than in the pale shadow Christianity had been reduced to in our time. Seen from his mystic eyes, the recent past looked all so petty — the ballet ban in the Fifties "because its skimpy costumes led to impure thoughts," the agonized hours we spent calculating when exactly kissing one's steady shaded from venial to mortal sin, the hellfire thundering in our retreat master's voice over "sins against chastity." Birth control, married priests, the ordination of women — today's burning issues — are mere variations on a theme to survivors of a patriarchal One True Church petrified by fear of God-created sap flowing in the veins of little schoolgirls and boys.

I closed the last page of *The Phenomenon of Man* with a silent whoop one unforgettable dawn in the early Sixties. That it could not be published in the author's lifetime only intensified the thrill. His Jesuit superiors had feared an inspiring new cosmology as much as the nuns had feared our youthful libido. Losing no time, I signed up into the global Teilhard de Chardin Society and proceeded to break the great news to my *barkada*.

By now they, too, had begun to feel the beginnings of a Great Thaw, confirmed by the radical vision of the roly-poly Angelo Cardinal Roncalli who became Pope John XXIII just as we entered college. With his "opening of the Church's windows and doors" in the Second Vatican Council came the reminder that "Catholic" means "universal." Its historic dialogue with other world religions, I noted with satisfaction, put Mother Superior in her place for all time.

A sea-change in consciousness

Irreverent colleagues on my first newspaper job found my long-standing habit of daily Mass strange indeed, their snickering echoed by a daily churning of news on violence, graft and corruption. The ideal of living *sub* s*pecies aeternitatis* — under the light of eternity — had begun to fade in a world crying for reform.

Soon it had refocused on the whys and wherefores of the ugliness that I was, it seemed, seeing for the first time. I was dumbstruck by a ubiquitous Filipino reality — a gun-toting, influence-peddling ruling class which not only seemed to be everywhere but also owned or held the option on everything the government, the Church and the United States of America did not lay claim to.

The last bricks of old convent walls had come tumbling down by the time I found myself in New York for graduate school in journalism in the mid-Sixties. I learned Marxism in the winds of my first winter and its rising tide of protest against the Vietnam War. With a silent sob, I began to understand the depth of my country's thrall to formidable alien powers within and without.

Surrounding me now were classmates who adorned their dorms with huge posters of Marx and Lenin, Students for a Democratic Society campaigning against the Vietnam War across the walk from Journalism School and an American boyfriend who studied Asian history and Mandarin while agonizing over dodging the draft by joining a Peace Corps he did not believe in. As naturally as breath came our identification with the Vietnamese people's struggle for sovereignty under the talons of an American Eagle whose claw-hold on the Philippines I could now measure *in situ.*

Politico-economic critique of the American military-industrial complex was made doubly riveting by the insight that the Judeo-Christian heritage underlay the history of modern colonialism. *Inang Bayan* as a mere source of cheap raw material and a market for finished products, a pawn in a global arms race and a setting for the proxy wars of a developed West. Such issues of Third World unfreedom marched before me like a parade of Halloween masks that winter in New York. "Cold War," the largest mask of all leered over a whole chunk of the modern history in which my lifetime had begun.

I was yet to hear of a prior choice in the matter when I began exploring options for navigating through a crazy mixed-up world where even God had just been declared dead. My first LSD trip in the late Sixties lived up to a promised opening of "doors to perception." But as the inner space it had illegally opened invited further exploration, there came a stronger call.

The revolution announced by the exuberant slogans of ballooning student demonstrations in Manila exerted a powerful counterpull. The fateful choice was between joining the brain drain with a cushy job in Manhattan, or helping earn freedom for a downtrodden native land. Soon after finishing the last of my degree requirements and a fond farewell to Greenwich Village, I booked a flight home to Manila, raring to jump into the maelstrom.

But first I had to examine the facts of those fascinating demonstrations as a proper journalist. One day, attendance at teach-ins and rallies to interview the ringleaders led to an unforgettable bus ride from the UP campus to a printing press somewhere in Caloocan with a young Jose Maria Sison who could find time for me only between revolutionary errands.

Joma was at his professorial best in our one-to-one teach-in on unjust structures ruled by "corrupt politicians, *comprador* bourgeoisie and clerico fascists puppeteered by the American military-industrial complex." In that heady moment of truth was also when I realized that it was one thing to shed ingrained anti-Communist bias and quite another to make ready to shed the blood of people I knew to make way for a "dictatorship" of farmers and laborers I had never met.

Joma's tolerant smile, as I confessed to the "limitations of my class origins in the face of a major historical task," disturbed me for a long time. With only my bibliophilia to offer a revolution that called for thought, word and deed, I jumped at a chance to interview the venerable Teodoro Agoncillo on his newly published *Revolt of the Masses*. Sympathy for his deconstruction of Philippine history could only deepen my guilt.

Thus did I find my place in the revolutionary roster of my generation as a sympathizer willing to provide overnight safehouses to braver compatriots, hide their subversive books and contribute material support. It helped that the ones I sheltered were colleagues in the media who could laugh at discomfiting revolutionary moments, like the time two of them wound up sleeping in a townmate's chicken coop when my frightened mother put her foot down against sheltering the Communist revolution in our home.

Thus did we live through a time of *maski-paps* — storms, floods and earthquakes accompanying citywide demos, strikes, mass arrests, sudden disappearances, the death and imprisonment of dear friends. An end to trouble was nowhere in sight. The Moro National Liberation Front had just launched its own version of revolution when another youth movement called "counterculture" invited everyone to "consciousness-expansion."

LSD, marijuana, metamphetamines and industrial strength-sedatives made an ironic path to consciousness crowded with addicts and escapists. Drug busts, deaths from overdose, nervous breakdowns only lengthened the list of friends and loved ones to mourn and comfort. Somewhere between the hospital basement, drug rehab center, funeral parlor and military camps would come the painful sobering.

Our generation's flashes of illumination had only brought us subtler contradictions beyond resolution by guns, drugs and political manifestos. The Vietnam War was ending with American withdrawal, the Communist revolution regrouping after its first debacle under martial law, a censored press was blacking out the facts behind a bleeding Mindanao as a new life syllogism slowly crystallized.

Our generation has demanded an end to all injustice, it went. Now it is embroiled in war both external and internal. Therefore, came the conclusion, our cry for change is empty unless we begin in the most crucial battlefield — not in "a neocolonial political system," not down Timothy Leary's path, but in both their foundations, our own hearts and minds.

The social historian William Irwin Thompson put a name to the new impulse — a "civilizational sea-change" emerging from growing global realization that old political, economic and cosmological systems, the Communist one included, had become insufficient for the deepest human needs. To decode a world in the complete dysfunction that has always preceded a new order, we first had to learn the basic premises of the system where our generation was crying — and dying — for change.

The root of the world *radical*, a generic description of this generation, is "radix" meaning root. Youthful imaginations released from fascination with outer revolution soon found their way to the roots of different spiritual traditions as the only material enduring enough for new ways of being. By now a decade of dust had gathered on my copy of Teilhard de Chardin's *The Phenomenon of Man*. As the burning eyes of a beloved French mystic stared back at me again, I could now stare back from the surer footing of experience.

In the pioneering Caliraya Foundation for Higher Consciousness and the Environment was where a new circle of life gathered in the fitful Seventies. There we slowly traced the entire legacy of a Western civilization that had colonized our country twice over, all the way to its taproot in the French Enlightenment. Its enthronement of human reason, once an *ilustrado* weapon against the obscurantist rule of Spanish friars, had combined into our own heritage of American colonialist lust and the selfish ambitions of a new Filipino elite. A fatal narrowing of focus was now strangling a burgeoning nation, systematically passed on to generation after generation, obscuring the wrong turning made soon after the Philippines' revolutionary birth a century ago.

This narrow focus had pockmarked all of twentieth-century Philippine history with agrarian revolts, now throwing multiplying city slums and beggars into the bargain.

Understanding how our modern misery began without joining the Communist armed struggle was, in its way, harder work. It meant dealing with the fact that both the heroes and villains of Philippine history were part of a contemporary consciousness alienated from its own deepest roots. Seeking an end to this agony through the twists and turns of the Seventies and Eighties was how a magical door gradually opened to our insistent knocking. It led right back to the tribal heart of our country. What is truly precious in our heritage, how it could help heal a generation at war with itself slowly became the object of a new mythical quest.

It often seemed tangential in a time of savage militarism but research into folk phenomena like faith healing was where the true nature of native giftedness long discredited in mainstream history first began to emerge before our eager seekers' eyes. The "counterculture" of *ilustrado* heirs aspiring to become *iluminados* had gone underground in its own fashion. There, in sweet homecoming, emerged layer upon layer of a much older Filipino reality — in indigenous concepts of land, agriculture, law, forestry, justice, marriage and healing, bringing new humility and a fresh understanding of what our race and nation might truly be if only we looked a little deeper.

New incarnations

"There are no accidents in the Universe" was one of the things the Caliraya years taught me. One evening in 1982, I provided casual company at the opera for my friend Arlene Babst and her friend, the publisher Hans Menzi. The next morning, the general made me a surprise offer to join Arlene as a columnist in the *Bulletin Today.* "Martial law's been lifted. It's a chance to speak up again," Arlene argued as I hesitated after a protest absence as old as P.D.1081. After two months of pussyfooting, I hesitantly agreed to return to the mainstream.

A by-line in the country's largest newspaper brought the next surprise — an invitation from the *Partido Komunista ng Pilipinas,* to my first trip behind the Iron Curtain for a "Global Assembly for Peace and Life" in Prague, a city of eerie soulfulness. The conference message brought me to near shock: the Soviet Union was tired of the arms race and now wanted peace with its American superpower rival.

A succeeding brief visit to Moscow brought a sneak preview of a new force about to emerge on the world stage. Our Filipino delegation was prepared for it by a panorama of Soviet history at the Tretyakov Gallery. There, before my widening eyes, peered a mystical soul from a huge and powerful wintry canvas of wild-eyed Russian peasants in Pentecostal procession. That evening, four members of the Soviet Peace Committee led by "a God-fearing Communist," the humorous head honcho Yuri Drozdov, came for dinner. How can I ever forget those three men in frayed coats, like three noblemen in disguise in the freezing winds of early Moscow spring straight out of Tolstoy, reiterating a Soviet desire to end the Cold War? They asked us to bring the message home to a Philippines a-spin in the US orbit.

Over two decades since the Voice of Democracy, my attempt to deliver this message brought another measure of the Cold War's deep trenches in our country. First I learned that my stories from Prague and Moscow had not seen print in General Menzi's newspaper. Ronald Reagan was coming for a state visit in two months around September of '82. In preparation, my three fellow-women columnists and I had just been fired — the *Bulletin Today* could not afford four unguided missiles in a newspaper where Marcos owned the controlling stock. Just as I had feared when I first said "yes" to Mr.Menzi, Arlene Babst, Ninez Olivares, Melinda Quintos de Jesus and I turned out to have been mere window-dressing to the "return of democracy" with the "lifting" of martial law in 1981.

My report on a new spirit behind the Iron Curtain was eventually published in another Menzi publication but it became a mere ripple in the media as new turbulence slowly came to a boil after ten years of media suppression under martial law. The highhanded padlocking of the feisty independent tabloid *We Forum* in 1982 provoked the first rally for press freedom since P.D.1081, led by four female *Bulletin* ex-columnists wearing mourning black in front of Camp Aguinaldo. This was followed by a second rally in Liwasang Bonifacio where equally flamboyant members of the local film industry made common cause with repressed colleagues in the print media on Valentine's Day '83.

Hearts were aflame as militaristic arrogance approached a climax provoked by the empowerment of the Board of Review for Motion Pictures to burst into preview rooms and burn master negatives of "subversive" films by the likes of Brocka, Bernal, Diaz-Abaya and Mike de Leon. The Marcos regime was setting itself a deadline it would recognize too late. In a trice, private eddies of protest converged into a whirlpool building up to a tidal wave. Next came a large meeting of activist organizations whose cries for a massive boycott of the "crony press" shook the rafters of the Heritage Art Gallery, now a nerve center for protest.

And then the times flipped over. News of the Aquino assassination crackled the very day after that huge boycott meeting, breaking a historical dam that carried our media outcry in a rising flood that, three unforgettable years later, swept the Marcos regime along with it. Old friends came floating from the underground straight to my living room. For a brief moment it seemed the activist and "hippie" strains of our generation were finally on the way to a shared breakthrough.

But no. As the new Cory government quickly laid waste our hopes by restoration of elite rule, old soulmates would once more be painfully parted as the militaristic legacy of the Marcos years next faced off with a rigidifying Filipino Communist ideology. The *pobres y ignorantes*, having once more given muscle to history as "people power," would return to the sidelines of history. The divided inner life of our revolutionary generation would have to continue playing itself out.

In time the world would witness the truth of our Soviet Peace Committee friends' words in the emergence of Mikhail Gorbachev. Delicious reversals of stereotypes had become global fashion by the time an American writer revealed that Gorby's grandmother had taught him to pray before the religious icons of old Russia in his youth. A time of new marvels was in full career when I accepted a second invitation to the Soviet Union two years after EDSA. Awestruck, I saw the Virgin Mary, just hoisted on the shoulders of a massive national upheaval in my country, hovering again over a celebration of the millennium of Christianity in the heart of the "evil empire." What strange new blessing was this — witnessing part of the message of Fatima fulfilled before the very eyes of a recycled Catholic?

That timeless moment continued a year later with an invitation to a journalists' tour of environmental programs in Germany, just as Gorbachev's *perestroika* was pulling the rug from under the entire Soviet Bloc back in Moscow. News of growing demos against East European Communist regimes had begun trickling out to the West as, one autumn Sunday in October 1989, I broke off from our official tour to peek into East Berlin where rumors hinted at interesting developments.

I received two surprise gifts at the Philippine embassy residence in the greying Communist half of Berlin: a tiny medallion of Our Lady of Lourdes and a painting of Poland's famous Lady of Schostakowa. *A capella* chanting of the "international *Ave Maria*" welcomed me to an unprogrammed visit to the Convent of Notre Dame de Vie where an EDSA veteran's happy suspicion was confirmed by breathless nuns: another liberation movement propelled by students, artists, workers and the Church was slowly coming to a climax behind the Wall.

The official visit was over but nothing could tear me away from a city in whose gaping wound of division I saw the face of my entire generation. Like an answer to a heartcry, on the front page of the *International Herald-Tribune* next emerged another haunting image of Our Lady standing with deep, compassionate eyes beside a West German chancellor embracing the prime minister of Communist Poland in reconciliation. Two days later, after a million-strong rally on East Berlin's Alexanderplatz, the Berlin Wall fell. My emerging new slant on nuns, convents and Virgins at the end of a long Cold War had just been fixed in amber.

Yes, I now track miracles into my fifth decade — not of the weeping statue genre but of the more invisible, enduring kind. There remains formidable resistance to my point of view but I have found a new home in the world of NGOs where the foundations of a new time, perhaps even a civilization, are being laid. With the recovered wisdom of the heart and a new reverence for Nature, here we listen to and amplify the voice of a silent majority whose real genius is yet to be heard in their amnesiac country.

It's hard work but the years have rewarded me with an energy-saving device: choosing the arenas of outer battle with things that need changing while keeping a sharp eye for their outposts inside myself. I have learned to be polite while hurling swords to target, twisting the blade when necessary — in love and blessing because it all paradoxically comes out even in the end.

I've also begun to "surrender the things of childhood" though at times I miss the dark-haired girl who once looked back at me from the mirror full of urgent questions, and think of dyeing my now salt-and-pepper hair black in a simulation of vanishing youth. Instantly the 24-year-old jazz musician, writer and martial artist who is my only child reminds me that life, if not the human body, remains forever young. "Don't!" he protests. "You look like an elf — a distinguished elf!"

Sweeter words a midlifer cannot hope to hear from a young man starting out on his own new quest beyond the convent walls of his mother's birthing.

The Meandering Mind of a
More-Than-Middle-Aged Matron
Solita Collas-Monsod

On Youth and Gender

THE YOUNG WOMEN of today are better off than those of my generation in one major sense. No, it is not because the former are living in the information age. We grew up with television and talking pictures, and our parents grew up with radio and silent movies — one expects this kind of technological progress. Rather, today's young women are better off, I think, because they are no longer held captive (not much, anyway) by the gender crap that was so much a part of the cultural and social environment of my generation. A specific example should illustrate what I mean.

A young friend, Giovanna Mabanta (she is as Filipina as they come, and yes, she calls me *Tita*), is married to a commercial photographer, a Spaniard. They are now living in London and are the parents of a beautiful baby girl. What makes Giovanna different from her counterpart of a generation earlier? A lot.

— For one, Giovanna (her nickname is Baby) married at 29. In my time, if a girl wasn't married by the time she was 22 or 23, she was considered an old maid, which was a source of worry and humiliation to parents and girl alike. Something must be wrong with her. The destiny of the female of the species was to get married and raise a family as soon as possible, so everything she was brought up to do was in preparation for this role. Not a few parents felt it was a waste of time to see a daughter through college — she was better off taking cooking and sewing classes.

At her wedding, Baby's mother and father marched with her down the aisle. This was not at all done in my generation. A small point perhaps, but significant. The implication then was that the father "owned" his daughter and thus had the right to "give" her away. The current practice signifies that both mother and father of the bride are escorting her to her new life.

— Baby, though married, has not changed her name. She is Giovanna Mabanta and she is married to Jose LasHeras. She is not Giovanna LasHeras. That would never have happened in my time, but it is becoming more and more common now. The practice of taking the husband's name is presumably part of this whole concept of being owned by the father and then given away by him to the husband. Woman as chattel. Odious, if one really thinks about it. I was brought up to accept without question this practice of giving up one's name, but the young women of today are not so easily persuaded, hopefully.

— Baby didn't have a baby right away — she planned it that way. In my time there was no choice. That's what a woman got married for — to have babies, and the sooner the better. If she didn't, something must be wrong with her.

— I save the best for last. Two and a half months after her baby girl was born, Giovanna, who is an industrial designer, had to travel from London to Milan on business. Did she take her baby with her? No. She left Adrianna with her husband Jose, who had no qualms or reservations about taking care of his daughter while Giovanna was away. From the beginning of their marriage, you see, Jose and Giovanna have been sharing the responsibilities of running the household and caring for the baby is also a shared responsibility — and delight. None of this me-Tarzan, you-Jane delineation of roles where the husband's "duty" is to provide the wherewithal and the wife's "duty" is to rear the children and take care of the home.

In this day and age, and perhaps perforce, both husband and wife are income earners, undertaking the so-called productive roles. It is but logical that they also share the reproductive roles, the caring for the home and rearing of the children.

While male chauvinists and most of those who were brought up in my generation may be horrified at this, what they don't realize is that the Jose LasHerases of this world are better off: they have the opportunity to bond in a very special way with their offspring and are rewarded with a better quality of family life because of it.

Luckily, in my generation I was among the fortunate who had very few gender restrictions constraining me.

I was lucky because I was blessed with parents who thought that an education — a good one — was the most important legacy they could leave their children, male or female (they didn't have very much choice, actually, because they had five daughters and only one son). Both my parents were ahead of their time with their concept of human capital development. My dad met my mom in New York. He was a journalist and she was a *pensionada*. This was in the late Twenties, you understand, when travel abroad for a young Filipina was a rare opportunity — and rarer still was the chance to take graduate studies abroad. But Mom had been given a scholarship to study social work at Columbia University and she did not at all hesitate to accept it. She was unique for her time in more ways than one — she married when she was 27 years old.

Obviously, then, I grew up in a family which was neither patriarchy nor matriarchy: my parents respected and consulted each other. My father did not (dared not?) treat my mother as chattel, that's for sure, although Mom had what is called the double burden: she helped Dad with the family finances because she worked, but running the household and rearing the children were also solely her responsibilities. I don't think it ever even crossed Dad's mind to lend a hand in household and child care activities. That just wasn't done.

I also had the great good luck to have married someone who doesn't have a single chauvinistic bone in his body. I admit, with shame, that it was I, rather than Christian, who was imbued with a sense of gender roles. And therein lies another tale.

Scarcely a month after our wedding, Christian and I went to the US for graduate studies. He was one of 12 successful applicants (out of 600), who were invited to join the World Bank as part of its first batch of junior professionals. A wonderful offer, and not to be turned down, but it meant moving to Washington, D.C., from Philadelphia. He did.

I remained behind to (a) have my second baby (remember what I said about no choice?) and (b) finish my course work for my Ph.D. and study for the comprehensive exams. But there was no question in my mind, although we had never even discussed it, that my career was subordinate to his. The gender dimension at work. Man — breadwinner; woman — homemaker. I was going to join him in Washington at the earliest opportunity. And I did, although my thesis adviser pleaded with me to remain at the university because, he said, once I left the academe, I could kiss my dissertation goodbye. (As it turned out, he was right.)

So I joined Christian in Washington and proceeded to set up a household with our two baby girls. And by heaven, I wanted to be the best possible housewife and homemaker. I was a most efficient one, too, if I may say so myself. I was inordinately proud of the fact that one could eat off my floors (although who would want to is beyond me), they were so clean. My girls were extremely bright babies and were the talk of the neighborhood because of their accomplishments. And somehow our apartment was the gathering place of the housewives who would break their morning chores for coffee and a little gossip.

Christian would come home to a sparkling clean apartment, with sparkling clean babies, and have a good meal prepared by a solicitous wife. My cup runneth over, I thought, An idyll even, I thought.

The idyll was rudely shattered by my husband. We were chatting over dinner — actually, it was I doing the talking, telling Christian about the latest neighborhood gossip, feeling not a little superior to the other wives, who were being beaten up or betrayed or just ignored by their husbands.

And then Christian dropped a bombshell. He very deliberately put down his fork and knife, and said, "Winnie, I think you'd better look for a job."

I was stunned. Had he been fired? Were we in desperate financial straits? Was something wrong with his health? All these rushed through my mind in the time it takes to draw a breath.

Christian explained, "Your mind is getting atrophied. I didn't marry you so I could come home and have you gossip to me about who beat up whom or who was unfaithful to whom, but this is all you can think or talk about. And it is not good for you. Or for me. So get out into the world and start expanding your horizons again. Get a job."

This, at a time when husbands expected their wives to stay home and felt it was humiliating to have their wives work (the "What-will-people-think? They-will-think-I-can't afford-to-support-you" mentality). And then, more likely than not, these selfsame husbands would have extramarital affairs because their wives bored them. And their wives, with no other options, i.e., means to support themselves, would be forced to take that kind of infidelity crap.

Christian had no such hang-ups. He was worried about me, as well as, of course, himself and our long-term relationship. And as I sat there, reliving in my head the empty prattle to which I was subjecting him, I knew he was right. So I went out the next day and started looking for a job.

How many husbands would think in this manner?

Christian had no hang-ups either about doing "reproductive" chores: changing the children's diapers, or bathing them, or feeding them, or giving them their medicine when they were sick — none of that "it's-your-job-not-mine" attitude. In fact, he enjoyed doing them, in contrast to a lot of our male friends who were proud to say they didn't know one bean about taking care of the children — that's what their wives and their *yayas* were for.

As I say, I was lucky.

Christian was lucky, too. His children adore him and are very close to him. When I am away from home, for example, one of the children will slip into our bedroom and spend the night on the couch. Not a word is said, but they all remember how once he had a *"bangungot"* — he jumped out of bed and hurt himself badly (he had to have stitches), and they want to make sure that doesn't happen again. I think he made his own luck.

On Marriage

Our marriage is considered, by a great many people, to be both happy (wanting what we get) and successful (getting what we want). But more important, it is considered so by the people whose opinion really counts — our parish priest, our children — the ones who know us most intimately, from whom practically nothing can be hidden.

Christian and I hold the same view. Put it this way: if I were to do it all over again, I would still choose him to be my partner for life. I'm not going to push my luck by asking him what he would do if we could push the clock back by 35-odd years. But one thing sure — we're not staying together because we have to, but because we want to.

To what do I attribute this felicitous state of affairs, i.e., what are the ingredients that contributed to our happy and successful marriage? Let me see now...

Friendship has to be a basic ingredient. Christian and I were friends, really good friends, before he decided to change the equation. He was an Upsilonian and his fraternity was very much into campus politics, and they asked me to run in their ticket for the college student council. Although I never asked why I had been chosen, I think they needed girls with good grades.

Christian and another Upsilonian fetched me from my home to take me to a preliminary meeting of the candidates. That was the first time we met. No rockets went off. No meaningful glances were exchanged. No pregnant pauses. Just a casual, pro forma "Hi, nice to meet you," and then on to the business at hand.

His looks were eminently forgettable. (Another meandering: It is so unfair. Men age so well — they become distinguished-looking while women just get either wrinkled or fat. Christian looks 10 times better now at 60 then he ever did when he was young.) Looking back over more than 30 years, a very dear friend of mine described how our respective husbands looked when they were single college men: average to *ugs* (i.e., ugly) closer to *ugs*. Her description was apt.

But even at our first meeting, I noticed he had a terrific sense of humor. He had a dry wit and an excellent sense of timing with his jokes and repartee. A good time was had by all.

Through the next two years, our friendship deepened. We enjoyed the banter, the easy companionship. With each other, there was no need to put on an act. We liked each other very much, without a single romantic overtone.

He enlisted my help in courting a very pretty girl that he had his eyes on, a sorority sister of mine. I'd tell him what movie we would be going to, and he would just "happen" to meet us there. I'm sure she was on to our stratagem but was too polite to mention it. Besides, she too was interested. Christian also enlisted my help in chaperoning them on dates as her aunt was very strict. I would accompany him to fetch her and he would very thoughtfully provide a date for me for the evening, usually a fraternity brother of his. When I would see Christian and his girl in deep whispered conversation with each other, I would turn to my date for the evening, lean over closer to him and whisper intimately, "Peter Piper picked a peck of pickled peppers," and we would break up laughing, to the intense curiosity of our tablemates. A good time was had by all.

I was Christian's confidante. And he was mine. He knew how I felt (repulsed) about the boys who had the temerity to try to court me — I was a very young 16 and 17. He witnessed me in the throes of my first serious crush — a boy (a man, rather, since he was six or seven years older), from a rival fraternity at that, who was also pursuing me. It was a mark of our great friendship that Christian made no belittling remarks about the fellow and in fact provided me with what I thought was wise counsel. He, too, served as my messenger boy when I needed to communicate with my crush, who lived in the dorm.

I don't know how he managed it, but Christian kept a straight face when I came to him with my great tale of romantic woe: my crush had asked my permission to kiss me the night before he left for summer vacation abroad, and I felt compelled to refuse indignantly, even if I was dying to experience that first kiss. I was afraid, you see, that I would "lose his respect" (see what kind of hang-ups girls were brought up to have in my time?). Why didn't he just kiss me, I moaned my complaint to Christian, the way it happens to other girls? Now, I would have to wait until summer was over.

As you can see, there was nothing we couldn't talk about. In the more than two years between the time we met and the time I became his girlfriend (yes, it was very sudden — there was no courting as such, only a very long discussion wherein he convinced me that I actually loved him but just didn't know it. After some reflection I concurred, and that was it. I became his girl), there were any number of dances we both attended but we never once danced with each other. We were buddy-buddy-old-pals and the thought never even occurred to me to want to dance with him.

To make a long story short, it was Christian who gave me my first kiss — and he didn't ask my permission, either. He wasn't about to make the same mistake my first crush did. Smart man.

Christian and I are still the best of friends. And that is very important. It is possible to betray a lover, I think, but it is extremely difficult to betray a friend.

Love is another main ingredient. At first blush, this seems rather trite. As the song goes, love and marriage go together like a horse and carriage. But I'm not talking about the can't-help-lovin'-that-man-of-mine variety. I'm talking about the long-haul, yes-I-can-help-lovin' variety. The love-is-a-decision as opposed to the I-fell-in-love situation. The distinction is that the former implies a control that is absent in a fall-in (as well as fall-out) situation. Frankly, I think that most marriages go on the rocks because the transition is never made from falling-in-love to loving.

Don't get me wrong. The decision to love does not involve gritting one's teeth and thinking "I-made-my-bed-so-now-I-must-lie-in-it." On the contrary, it is an "I-made-my-bed-and-I-WANT-to-lie-in-it-with-him" scenario. The difference is in the perspective. Here is how it works — with us, anyway. Anytime there is a low point in the relationship, or preferably even if there is none, think of all the things that are attractive about your partner and what attracted you to him in the first place. Accentuate the positive. And when the urge to merge fades, we follow Fr. Chuck Gallagher's advice: Pray for PASSION. And follow it up with working for it. Think or do or say anything that is going to get that passion level up. Take it from me: there will never be a dull moment and the potential for new discoveries is enormous.

Two very good friends were discussing another lady in my presence. Apparently, the lady had just ended her third significant relationship (her first husband died, and the second and third marriages collapsed under the weight of the squabbles among their respective children, who couldn't stand each other). One friend divulged that she had advised the lady to stop trying for a permanent relationship, and just to date, if she needed escorts. My other friend agreed. "After all, at our ages sex is no longer important," she said. I disagreed vehemently with that assertion. "Speak for yourself, girl," I said. "Of course it is important. What's with you? You think a woman of 60 who needs a man is some sort of pervert, but you think it is normal when a man pushing 65 or 70 marries a woman 30 years his junior."

Maybe that was the feminist in me talking. Anyway, we had a good laugh. And she half-sheepishly and half-proudly admitted that her husband was still quite virile (he is past 70). She wasn't quite ready to admit, unfortunately, that she enjoyed it. But what's there to be ashamed of?

Which brings me to the last, and certainly not the least, of the main ingredients. GOD. This is not a goody-two-shoes, pro forma statement, I hasten to add. Here's what I feel about it: The love between husband and wife is the closest one can get on the human level to the love that God bears for us (this from Father Chuck, a Jesuit who heads the Matrimonial Renewal Center in New Jersey, which is behind the Parish Renewal, Evenings for the Engaged, Evergreen Antioch, Luke 18 and Marriage Encounter experiences, as well as from the noted author Fr. Andrew Greeley). So I would guess He has got more than a passing interest in keeping this love alive and growing. Therefore, calling on Him to give us passion is a logical step, as is calling on Him for checking in purposes, particularly when all else fails. I'm sure it has been said more elegantly elsewhere, but this is the best I can do: He'll come through.

Aside from the main ingredients, there are some "optionals" as well as suggestions for seasoning. In our case, one "optional" that turned out very well was that we started married life on our own. I mentioned earlier that we were married barely a month before we both left for the US. But even before we left, despite the knowledge that we would soon leave for abroad, we chose to rent an apartment and live apart from our parents after the wedding. This was on the advice of my "Aunt Doreen," no blood relative but an Englishwoman who was very close to the family, and it was one of the best pieces of advice we ever received or followed.

Because we were on our own and far away from well-intentioned relatives, we couldn't ever take the easy way out in an argument and run back to parents for tea and sympathy and possibly temporary shelter. We had to face the situation squarely and resolve it, as we had no one but each other to turn to. It's amazing how fast differences can be solved when one's negotiating arena is the matrimonial bed.

Another "optional" that strengthens our relationship is shared values. We both think honesty is the best policy (although Christian is much more tactful than I am). We both abhorred the Marcos dictatorship and did everything we could do restore democracy (in this undertaking, we were both proud and humbled when our children shared our concern and worked with us). We both feel that our marriage and our family are at least as important, and deserve at least as much attention, as our respective professions. Making "*lagay*," no matter how subtly done, is anathema to us. And any decision that affects the family would have to pass the test of our children's regard.

Finally, a sense of humor — the ability to laugh at oneself and with each other — has also played a very important role in our staying together, and more important, in enjoying each other's company. It is an important seasoning in our relationship. I'm not saying that every quarrel has ended in uproarious laughter. That would be farthest from the truth. We've had some real doozies — the knock-down, drag-out type of fights, figuratively speaking, of course — complete with the dreaded silent treatment. But these have been few and far between, thank the Lord. A good deal of potential trouble has been deflected by a pun here, a self-deprecating one-liner there. I have to admit that Christian is very much better at this than I am. I'd be in full flight, discoursing over some real or imagined hurt, and a remark from him would tickle my funnybone, and I'd start to laugh. And some sense of perspective would return.

I chuckle every time I remember a recent interview we had with a young lady for a TV special for Valentine's Day. I suppose we looked rather ancient to her, and when we said that God was very much a part of our marriage, she nodded her head sagely and said, "Your relationship must be very spiritual." Quick as a flash, Christian retorted, with an absolutely deadpan expression; "We also get very physical." After a moment of stunned silence, everyone present broke into laughter. The poor interviewer was embarrassed, but also, I think, quite thrilled.

...and Aging

She's pretty well-preserved for her age. That thought went through my mind when I caught my first glimpse of *Washington Post* publisher Katharine Graham more than 30 years ago. She was standing at the head of the stairs leading to the Sheraton Park Ballroom in Washington, D.C., patiently waiting in line to be received by Ferdinand and Imelda Marcos and US President Lyndon Baines Johnson. The occasion was a reception given by the Marcoses for Johnson in the course of the former's state visit to the US.

Mrs. Graham carried herself with great dignity and although she wasn't really pretty (Imelda Marcos' beauty was at its height and so everyone suffered in comparison), she was striking. Maybe it was the aura of power surrounding her that was so compelling. After all, the publisher of the most important daily in Washington was not so easily ignored.

But I meander. (Don't say I didn't warn you, though. Just look at the title of this piece.) The point is that as far as I was concerned, being myself all of 26 years of age at the time, the lady was OLD — as in venerable, as in ancient — when in fact she wasn't even 50. Ah, the arrogance of youth.

Amazing how that perspective changes. When I was in college, alumnae in their late thirties and early forties would attend our sorority gatherings, and we the resident sisters would look upon them with awe: so old! Now the shoe is on the other foot. I go to sorority gatherings with the resident sisters and they treat me as if I were about to break. I can almost hear their collective gasp when they are told that I joined the sorority 40 years ago.

I don't feel any older, you understand. It doesn't really sink in that I am older now than Katharine Graham was then. I still see myself, in my mind's eye, as a young woman. Actually, even when I face a mirror, I am so used to my face that I don't really see myself, if you know what I mean. And when I make remarks about my advanced age to my students in class, it is in the nature of a joke — to me anyway — although I am not sure they take it as a joke.

Sometimes, though, I am caught unawares and I see myself as others must see me. Like when I pass by a shop window, or an unexpected mirror, and catch my reflection. Then I get shocked at the lines and the bags and the wrinkles, and the bulges that the image reveals. How did I get so old? Or even, where did all these unsightly things come from?

Or I meet an old man or an old woman, only to find out that the person is my age, or even younger. That's when I have to accept that perhaps I look that old, too.

The pits, though, is when someone I consider middle-aged calls me "*Tita*." Or when the younger generation rush over to take me by the elbow and practically want to carry me to wherever I am going. That's when it hits me hard: *tempus fugit*. I do look old.

But I stoutly maintain that mine is not a case of refusing to "grow old gracefully." It's just that I don't FEEL or THINK old. I've been teaching for 25 years and when I look at my students, it doesn't seem as if the age gap now is any different from what the age gap was then. It's the people in front get the jar.

I'm not alone in this perception, by the way. My women friends tell me the same thing. So it must be natural — some form of psychological protection—to think of oneself as, well, not old. Something I read in a card somewhere describes exactly how I feel about myself: Young at heart, slightly older in other places. That's not so bad, is it?

This feeling is not limited to the female of the species. Recently, when my daughter and her fiancé were planning their wedding, they said they didn't want formal seating at the reception, only "bar tables" so that guests could mix around, and about eight or ten regular tables with chairs for the "oldies." Christian was genuinely puzzled that so many of those seats were needed. There were very few grandparents, after all, so who would be sitting there? I had to remind him that he and I, among the others, would be sitting there. *We* were the "oldies" my daughter and her fiancé had in mind. Christian was crushed for a little while, until the humor of the situation hit him and we ended up laughing about it.

So if I am as well preserved now as Katharine Graham was 30 years ago, I would consider that an achievement. That is my only concession to this aging process, aside from the fact that I now no longer bother to hide my age. Pretty soon, I guess, I will be thinking of the advantages of being 60 and over. I may not look forward to it, but I shan't fight it, either.

As the saying goes, "You can't help getting older, but you don't have to get old." Who knows? It may be that the best years are yet to come.

Spirit from Under-the-Ground

CRISTINA JAYME MONTIEL

LET ME TELL you some stories. After 45 years, I can speak of memories. And to get a little bit more organized, I shall divide my "life" into seven-year segments. They say that seven is a magical number, and as powerful as seven capital sins, seven-year itches, 77 forgiven transgressions. But that is going too far ahead. Let's start from the very beginning.

I was born in 1951, the fifth of eight children, in Sacred Heart Hospital in Paco, Manila. My parents were both medical doctors who worked for the Philippine government. I grew up feeling that we were intelligent but impoverished. My family resided in the Bulatao clan's house in Paco, with my maternal grandparents, grandaunts, uncles, aunts, cousins. I lived under one roof with around 30 relatives and shared a room with three sisters and two brothers.

I enjoyed the company of my siblings and cousins. We played *tirador, patintero, piko,* pick-up-sticks, jackstones, Scrabble and canasta. We also had pretend games. My cousin Gerry impersonated a priest. He would don a cape of white bedsheet, cut up bananas and give us "communion," use a badminton racket as a screen when we "confessed" to him. Gerry eventually entered the seminary but left after four years. He became a peasant organizer. During martial law he was arrested and badly tortured. He was saved from the electric shock treatment only because the power supply was unexpectedly cut off during his interrogation ordeal in Samar.

My parents called me a long-play record. I cried a lot, for hours on end. When my sisters and brothers took toys away from me, I would cry, unable to get my toys back. Dad said I was Miss Helpless. When I was told to do something which didn't meet my favor, I would refuse, get scolded and cry. Thirty years later, during my initial feeble attempts at therapy, my Mom told my therapist, "Tina seemed to have a mind of her own, even as early as two years old. She did not follow what we told her to do. She would just decline, then cry. At seven years, she stopped her crying and began having asthma attacks."

Slowly, I crafted a world of my own inside me, separate from the hustle and bustle of an overcrowded family home. Unable to fight for my own toys, I spurned authority.

In 1958, my family moved out of Paco and into a new, more spacious home in Cubao, Quezon City. I missed my grandmother very much. I was her favorite grandchild, or so I felt. I thought of how she read me bedtime stories, combed my hair, rubbed Vicks on my chest when my coughing got bad. I remembered the smell of her hair which had been washed in coconut oil. And her singing. To me she was perpetual music and cooking — singing while preparing *panada, batutay, inutukan* and other Pangasinan delights.

I began going to elementary school at St. Theresa's in Manila. I was utterly uncomfortable with what I felt was my family's pressure to be the best in everything. So my asthma attacks became more frequent. I found good excuse to be an academic underperformer. I ended up with the best-in-religion medals and "only" second honor awards. I just didn't enjoy school, especially the classroom competitions and meaningless memorizing. Oh yes, I liked my friends. We played warball, bought ten-centavo Cokes at recess, drowned our fried *lumpias* in vinegar. We giggled about our College Day crushes.

With a larger home in Cubao, I gained more private space. This I enjoyed. I spent hours on end lying in bed daydreaming. I invented fairy tales and songs in my mind. I also repeatedly thought of how lonely I was, but I didn't understand where all the loneliness was coming from.

I began writing poetry in my early adolescence. Please listen to me. My poems are the repository of my fragile soul. "The White Dove" and "In Dire Need of Comfort" reflect my adolescent insecurity and loneliness.

The White Dove

the white dove
flutters from its nest,
out into the world.
the world

sees the white dove
and frowns at its awkward flight.
the white dove
looks up —
and falls in love
with the waves of white clouds.
she looks around —
and appreciates herself;
> *for the silent trees are lovely*
> *for the blue lake is serene*
> *for her fellow doves are wonderful.*
the white dove
zooms up
and kisses the soft sky.
the world
sees the white dove
and smiles.

1964-1966 (13-15 years old)

In Dire Need of Comfort

darkness blankets the city
everything is still
and silent.

my soul, harken —
listen to the stillness of the night
let the darkness enfold you.

do not worry
do not squirm in restlessness
harken —
and be silent
and go to sleep.

1964-1966 (13-15 years old)

The years 1965-1972 were my time of political and sexual
revolutions. As a sophomore in high school, I helped organize a sitdown
strike to protest the deteriorating service in the cafeteria. We brought out

our lunches and sat along the school corridors. In junior high school I was elected class president and began going to dance parties every weekend.

I was recruited into a youth nationalist group called SPECC (Students for Political, Economic and Cultural Change) organized by Fr. Jose Blanco, S.J. We met regularly and talked about the growing unrest in the country, the scandalous gap between the rich and the poor, the corruption of the Marcos government. We also developed crushes on each other. I was attracted to Tony. After we held hands, I confessed my sin to our high school chaplain. He told me to pray one Our Father and three Hail Marys. I was 15. In my late teens, my social life became increasingly more colorful and I stopped going to confession. At 18, I knew love in all its youthful splendor. But in the midst of this explosive first love, I sought something more than noontime romance. I wrote "To Lovers at Noontime."

To Lovers at Noontime

A glance, a kiss to titillate,
And in my eye a girlish swoon,
Ye fools, go on — let none abate,
The glitter of the dream at noon.

Enjoy the wetness of earth's youth,
Of naked green and blushing gold,
The years will soon make rough the smooth,
And then perhaps we shall grow old.

But then, my love, where is the smile —
In yonder lips or 'neath the soul,
The cheeks do wrinkle and beguile,
The pretty masks that lose control.

So chomp the wine flasks all to bits,
Till glass turns sharp and laughter moans,
Till earth cries out midst screaming grits,
The horror of our cold dead bones.

And only then when noons corrode,
When dancing suns hide back in fright,
Shall mind and heart and soul explode,
Midst all the glory of the night.

October 1969

I plunged deeper into political activism. My organization KASAPI assigned me to work with the student front as recruiter, political educator and propagandist. I graduated from Maryknoll College with an A.B. in sociology, barely making cum laude. The evening of my graduation, I gave my medal to my parents, then went off to a weekend political seminar with urban poor leaders. In February 1972, I met and fell in love with Boyet, a community organizer in Escopa, Project 4. Martial law was declared in September 1972. Boyet was arrested and tortured. Upon his release from prison in December 1972, we got married.

In 1976, I gave birth to my beloved son Andoy. From then on, I felt complete. Andoy was, is and always will be my ultimate fulfillment.

I lived in two worlds. In one, there was the growing ruthlessness of martial law: massacred comrades, terrifying paranoia of intelligence agents, utter lack of privacy when political friends came in and out of my home, political plots and counterplots. In my other world, there was this magical symbiosis with Andoy: breastfeeding him with my endless supply of mother's milk, lullabying him to sleep, shooing away mosquitoes as he slept, being soothed by the music of his sparkling laughter. Amid the growing tensions of martial law, I found restful solace in Andoy.

It was also during these years that I began graduate school in Ateneo's psychology department. I got my master's degree in psychology in 1978, then I joined the faculty of the department.

My marriage was swiftly crumbling at the same time that political conditions in the country were deteriorating rapidly. I felt like I was being tossed here and there in a terribly chaotic storm. My poems cried out in pain. I turned into Wine on My Altar, fermenting and bloody.

Wine on My Altar

I will harvest
My grapes full of wrath
Put them one by one
In my barbed basket,
 Mournfully woven
 From prison wire
 Emblazoned by fire.

I will press
My grapes full of wrath
Squeeze them one by one

With my clenched fist,
Fingers clutching
Tortured fragments
Of dead comrades' garments.

Then I will wait,
Second by infinite second,
Nourished by bread broken.

I will offer
My wine full of wrath
Bless it drop by drop
In my own cup:
    A crimsoned chalice
    Painfully carved
    By goodness starved.

                       January 27, 1984 (33 years old)

Externally, I functioned with automated efficiency as an outstanding political and intellectual robot. Internally, I was torn between joining the armed struggle against the worsening dictatorship and remaining aboveground to take care of Andoy. Either choice demanded a high personal price. My womanness, my softness, surrendered to the turmoil. I literally grew a benign tumor in my entire reproductive system. My body again took over as spokesperson of my sadness. No seven-year-old asthmatic whimpers this time, but one big uteral primal scream. Before my thirtieth birthday I lost my womb, my own incarnate cradle of God's creation. "Virgin Birth" expresses the depths of my internal struggles as political and personal circumstances pressured me to make double-edged choices.

Virgin Birth

With guerrillas
She went
And spent
Nine years
On knees bent,
Blessed
By the deity
Of political purity.

She refused
The pressing offer
Of her lover
To touch
The cadre's trigger.

Pleased,
The Spirit moved
Within her
And she grew
Bigger.

Until her unborn
Was born
Crippled.

September 8, 1988 (37 years old)

During these years, I began my doctoral studies in social psychology and continued to be on the psychology faculty. I threw myself passionately into quantitative methods. I obsessively studied and taught all sorts of multivariate statistics in the psychology department: factor analysis, multiple regression, canonical correlation, discriminant analysis. I desperately needed some sense of structure and predictability in my emotionally anarchic life, and equations served that purpose. Beneath all this mathematical compulsiveness boiled turmoil.

When the Pilipino Democratic Party (PDP) was launched in 1982 in Cebu City, I participated in the congress as one of its active founding members. For the next ten years I was an ideological stalwart of the party. I went around the country giving grassroots basic recruitment seminars and political trainers' training. I wrote about structural analysis and drafted election campaign platforms. I jumped into the nerve center of political intrigues.

My person split into two oh-so-contradictory segments: streetwise political operations on one hand, and an anesthetized academia on the other.

And out of a fusion of chaos and order, years later, I have evolved my own sense of complexity.

Martial law ended with the 1986 People Power Revolution. The moment Marcos helicoptered to Hawaii, there was dancing in the streets. Andoy was ten years old then. He and I and my sister Susan's family drove to EDSA where rejoicing was at its peak. Andoy sat body out on the window of our car, obviously ecstatic. In EDSA, we danced and hugged the celebrating pressing crowd and screamed lustily from the pit of our stomachs. Andoy was so excited he developed a nosebleed. We went home that evening exhausted. I put some ice on Andoy's nose and he slowly fell asleep.

Because of the People Power Revolution, my husband Boyet was released from his third stint as a political prisoner. He had been behind bars since 1980. In the new democracy he joined the Quezon City local government and became a powerful Lord of the Flies. Our marriage crumbled beyond repair. Almost simultaneously the Russian Empire imploded. Socialist dreams shattered: the Red Sea parted. My interpersonal and ideological paradigms for meaningfulness collapsed.

I fell into a darkness that made me believe in hell. I felt cold and dead. I walked the desert of meaninglessness and emptiness, disjointed from any sense of a promised land. I grew numb all over. I lost all feeling — no political fervor, no passion for equations, no softness for Andoy. In hell there is no heat, only cold and hardness.

In 1989, I started psychotherapy at Ateneo's Center for Family Ministries. I trusted my therapist. He was a sensitive and capable psychologist who had worked with church-based urban poor organizations. I felt he understood my political involvements and handled my vulnerabilities with care. Shortly after I began therapy, I asked Boyet to leave the house. It was a very hard thing to do. My tear ducts worked overtime, caressing the dents of my woman-soul. I found it excruciatingly painful to accept that my 18-year marriage was over, perhaps never really existed beyond political pragmatism. And that I too had contributed to its decadence.

As I write this, I recall how my family provided the love and support I needed to get me through this crisis. Like many other families, mine is as flawed as imperfect can be. I have caused and received from them much pain. But when push came to shove, my parents and siblings were there, solidly supportive and caring. To them I offer my heartfelt gratitude. Mom and Dad gave me lots of positive emotional space to go through my feelings on my own. My sister Jayjay talked of the possibility of a research job in her Sociometrics Corporation in Los Altos, California. Eddie listened, smiled and accepted. My brother Bobby threw unprintable statements at my ex. He expressed for me things I could never have said myself. From Washington, D.C., Teejay constantly phoned and let me call her collect. We spent long woman-hours on the phone. Becky, Susan and Trixie were steadily beside my son and myself as we struggled to get up again. Gradually, so utterly slowly, Andoy and I began to stand on our own two feet in spite of the turbulence, the shock and the imagined social embarrassment of having a "failed family life."

At some awful moment in therapy, when I seemed emotionally paralyzed and couldn't move on, my therapist suggested that I consider going on a weekend spiritual retreat. I sought spiritual direction at the Cenacle Retreat House. In my first weekend retreat my spiritual guide recommended Psalm 23, about the Good Shepherd. I got stuck with the phrase "on restful waters" and kept thinking I wanted to swim in the Cenacle pool. When I shared this with my spiritual director, she encouraged me to go swimming. I swam the whole weekend and returned to work on Monday fully refreshed. Thus began my spiritual journey.

I am much indebted to my spiritual guide for her gentle and loving Jungian proddings. In my seven years with her, she has moved me through readings and introspections that helped me reclaim my positive sense of self, my sense of woman. These are the books I reflected on during my spiritual retreats. They are arranged in the order by which I took them in through the years: The Bible's *Book of Job*, Joyce Ruppe's *Praying Our Goodbyes*, Scott Peck's *The Road Less Traveled*, Clarissa Pinkola Estes' *Women Who Run with the Wolves* and Rainer Maria Rilke's *Letters to a Young Poet*. My spiritual growth has likewise been nurtured by colleagues in Ateneo's psychology department. Through their kind sharing, I have been able to read other Scott Peck books, Thomas Moore's *Soulmates* and *Care of the Soul*, and James Whitefield's *The Celestine Prophecy*.

In conjunction with my Jungian spiritual growth, I have kept a journal of my dreams. Here is my first dream-journal entry. I wrote it right after I began psychotherapy. It screams of raging jealousy and political machiavellianism.

My Dream, December 1989

There is a thin scraggly woman with her hands tied up high to a tree bough, and her feet bound. I am very angry and jealous of her. Boyet says, "No, no, she's just a Communist slave."

Here is another dream a year later. By this time, my internal self had come to terms with the reality of separation. This is a picture of blankness and the absence of human encounter (back to back sheets).

My Dream, November 1990

Two blank sheets of bond paper come together, back to back. One sheet is smooth, the other rough-grained. Then they become one sheet of paper and move horizontally in space. Then they separate again. I feel that the smooth sheet of blue paper is telling the other paper, "This is our separation."

Another year later — after crying gallons of pained tears, after cursing God and the rest of the human race, after seasons of social isolation and biting hostility — I start to heal. As shyly and quietly as new light softens a weary night, my natural inner spirit begins to radiate. My poetry remains heavily political, but becomes gentler, stronger, more illuminating. In "*Mahiyaing Hamog*" (Shy Morning Dew), I write about my quiet strength at the break of light.

Mahiyaing Hamog	Shy Morning Dew
Mahiyaing hamog *Sa bukangliwayway.*	Shy morning dew At break of light.
Gisingin ang manok *Kailangan tumilaok.*	Summon the rooster Crow for all others.
Patibayin ang bundok *Magtago sa tuktok.*	Forest the mountain - Hide there again.
Kalungin ang kasama *Hapos sa pakikibaka,*	Cradle the comrade, Weary and sad.
Wasakin ang dilim *Pag-asa'y malalim.*	Shatter the darkness With hope's caress.
Mahiyaing hamog *Sa bukangliwayway.*	Shy morning dew At break of light.

January 23, 1991 (40 years old)

Allow me to end this chapter with another dream. I am on the brink of recovery. In spite of the night, I discover the loving protection of the Evening Moon, and I feel safe.

My Dream, February 1991

A voice that is low and gentle talks inside my ear, direct to inside my head. It says, "In the shelter, in the shelter of the moon you will play."

In the past four years (1992-1996), I have emerged from my protective dark cave and reentered social life, renewed and integrated.

I continue my political activities but do so in a more reflective, low-key and open-hearted way. I have grown comfortable with my limitations and talents in relation to political work. These are the things I cannot do. I buckle down under stressful field operations. I'm too soft, transparent, insecure and impatient for wheeling-and-dealing assignments. Because of my high need for private space, I become imbalanced during prolonged seasons of public life. I cannot rabble-rouse. And what can I contribute? I can reflect. I can write. I can take on pedagogic functions. I can feel with others in pain and in joy. I can relate comfortably to individuals across varying positions of social influence. I am not easily affected by power or money. I have also come to terms with my all-too-human needs for affection, recognition and identity. So I am careful about when and how I satisfy these needs in the political arena. I have developed my own boundaries of pleasure without guilt.

I have likewise come to terms with my intellectual abilities. For so long, I had a love-hate relationship with the intellectual in me. Perhaps because of my rebellion against family pressure to achieve, perhaps because of my need to conform to the anti-intellectual culture of my activist groups. Today I have accepted what I want and do not want to do vis-à-vis intellectual work. I do not want: to memorize, to accept without checking out congruence with truth, to speak without meaning. I want: to observe, read, reflect, compute, write and teach. These give me much pleasure.

I have other needs as well. I need to have a community of friends. To nurture warm relationships with men and women alike who share similar intellectual and social interests. I have found a few authentic friendships in and out of Ateneo University. I need to be mentored. I pay tribute to my high school English teacher Lorna Kalaw-Tirol whose 25-year friendship has nurtured me through good and bad years. I am grateful to her for believing in my ability to write, even during those dark days when my soul disconnected with my pen.

My academic career has befriended my political passions. I no longer feel split into two different personalities. I am a political psychologist and a peace psychologist.

At the moment, my mind is full of questions about politics and peace. What are the humanizing elements of political involvement? Can men and women who jump into the nexus of politics protect themselves from the destructive elements of worldly power? In new democracies and Third World countries, do the roads to social justice, freedom and peace need to intersect perpendicularly? I am aware that there is so much social energy in politics. Like other forms of energy, politics can be either destructive or life-giving. Its contribution to social transformation has significant multiplier effects that can do tremendous good for communities, regions, nations. I have great respect for women and men of peace who have dared to travel the difficult path of pragmatic politics — Cory Aquino and Nene Pimentel, for example.

During my one year at the Peace Research Centre of The Australian National University in Canberra, I grew into the community of Canberra Quakers. I joined the Quakers for spiritual weekends and Sunday meetings for worship. I continue to keep in touch with them. I have been granted academic visits to different countries and have met other international colleagues with strong minds and loving hearts. I taught political psychology in Xiamen University, China, and did research on personality traits of conflict resolvers in seven societies while at the Technical University of Chemnitz-Zwickau in Germany. Connected by e-mail and occasional conferences, I am part of a burgeoning community of peace psychologists. Our intellectual and personal relationships break down state and cultural barriers. I am also with a subgroup called Women and Peace, an informal community of women (and one man!) psychologists bound together by our common dream of a peaceful world.

The varied involvements of my colleagues in political and peace psychology in different parts of the world are inspiring. Here are some examples of their positive works: in South Africa, post-trauma therapy with those who testify for the Truth and Reconciliation Commission; anchoring a political radio program in Peru; training in Gandhi's nonviolent methods in India; problem-solving workshops among influentials in Israel and Palestine; conflict resolution between Aboriginal and white Australians; research on narcoviolence in Colombia; understanding the nature of inner city violence in Washington, D.C.; and in North Ireland, examining the effects of war on children.

My own research interests include topics like citizen-based peacemaking in a protracted war; bargaining for peaceful termination of unsuccessful coup attempts; social psychological dimensions of resolving political conflicts. I am currently doing collaborative work with a Canadian political psychologist on the ethics of international development aid.

Although I continue to carry out my work conscientiously, I admit I have lost much of my sense of adolescent omnipotence, ideological righteousness and need to occupy political centerstage. With the fading away of these flames, I am left with a steadier and more focused kind of light.

May I share with you one more poem? Through "An Afternoon Prayer" I honor my colorful past and open myself up to a grace-filled future. I accept the cloud of unknowing.

An Afternoon Prayer

To onward move, will I
In spite the afternoon,
Small strength from memories
Of clarities at noon.
Oh where went they I ask
Ideologies complete?
Omnipotence was mine
Against the armored street.

Today I try to speak
But mumble out of stage,
Where once crowd microphones
Screamed out my righteous rage.

There is no red I feel
In heart that once was sweet,
No bravery to flaunt
As urban cadres meet.

The rigid line succumbs
Contorted and askew
Accepting strength from friends
As color changes hue.

In joyful dance curve I
Midst silence beyond bark,
As exclamation point

November 19, 1995 (44 years old)

My son Andoy turns 20 this year. He is a junior college student at Ateneo. Our mother-son relationship changes constantly as both of us grow older. To me, he is a beautiful spirit — gentle, open-hearted, clear-minded, curious, and with a contagious sense of humor. He knows that whatever he becomes or does, my love for him will remain constant and strong. I take great joy in watching him go his own way. There are times I wince when he stumbles. Or when he makes decisions different from how I would have made them.

Andoy is no longer afraid of the dark. When he was four years old, while we were hiding from the military in the forests of Bukidnon, he developed night phobia. But he is more confident of himself today. I suppose along the years, in his own special way, he too has confronted his own fears. So he sleeps soundly tonight.

When I was a two-year-old, I began crafting an internal world of my own. Even today I find myself taking lengthy excursions into my lively interior self. This puzzling, protective, productive inner-world absorbence I still do not comprehend fully. There are times when the inward attraction of my subjectivities becomes very strong. I occasionally exert conscious effort to remain connected with the practical demands and responsibilities of day-to-day living. I suppose people whom I relate to or work with sometimes sense that I am not "with them." It is in this private world where I reflect on past experiences, envision my future, wrestle with my angst, caress my soft heart, play with words and ideas, create poetry.

Like Andoy, I sleep soundly at night. And I continue to dream. I have learned to accept that dreams bring nightmares. And that dreams carry illuminating visions, too.

This is where my story ends. Or begins.

High on Midlife

BOOTS ANSON ROA

I LOOK at the mirror a little more intently this fine Sunday morning and capture the following in glaring truth:

51 years capsuled in my 5'6 1/2" and 135-pound frame — a 10-pound increase over the last 15 years;

a woeful tale of the tape, i.e. two atrocious inches added to the waistline and the hips;

two unwanted layers of flab on the abdomen, matched by mini versions under the chin;

eyebags that threaten to grow into suitcases;

crow's-feet metamorphosing into a maze;

neck rings that may soon spiral; and

gray hair under that glamorous Clairol sheen.

The situation is ostensibly tragic, enough to elicit a shriek and spawn a bout with depression!

Ten years back, I would have resorted to compulsive eating after such wretched reminders staring me in the face. But the years have shifted my focus.

And so the following self-assurances instead:

The crows-feet are actually, ehem, laugh lines.

With neck rings, who needs a choker and a pendant?

Whether eyebags or suitcases, who cares? They're Gucci quality.

No Clairol on the hair = the salt and pepper look: sexy, distinguished, even enigmatic.

Finally, with the added weight, inches and layers, there's really more of me to love, huh, Pete?

Pete dishes out an almost perfunctory but approving smile. The years have added weight, inches and layers to my life; his smile has added life to my years.

Through the years, our collective smiles have graduated into laughter, becoming more and more constant, free, wholehearted ... even passionate.

This is midlife's greatest gift to Pete and me: the gift of laughter. We laugh at comedians' staple — the funnies in print, on radio and television. We laugh at genuine capers on film.

We laugh at our children's stories, local and international (we have one child here and three in the US). We laugh at our grandchildren's antics, both "*gracia*" and "*desgracia.*"

We laugh at our follies and mistakes, but not quite at the mistakes of others. Instead we laugh at how some take themselves too seriously — at the workplace, at the rostrum or the pulpit, on and off camera, on the dancefloor, at the screen test, the beauty contest, the macho contest.

We laugh as we bemoan the innocent children who experience feigned and fleeting glory during those harrowing "Little Miss" or "Little Mister" contests — perfect forums for their stage mothers, stage fathers, stage *lolos* and *lolas*, and, not to forget, their stage managers and PROs.

I laugh at myself after a good cry at the movies. I laugh at myself when the maid points to my long-lost car keys in the refrigerator's vegetable compartment; or when I wash my face with my eyeglasses on; or when I put a string around my finger and forget what the string stands for; or when nobody laughs at my joke ... or when my listeners berate me after I explain it.

I laugh when I develop gas pains because I laugh too much. I even laugh when I hear unusual or hilarious laughter. It is true, laughter – and the joy it elicits – is infectious.

Laughter at midlife differs from my laughter during high school, or college, or even the earlier years of my career. Laughter then was occasionally at the expense of others. Now it is often even at my own expense, but minus rancor and bitterness. Laughter now is kinder, both to myself and to others.

The gift of laughter springs from optimism: the capacity to see the good in whatever comes our way. I remember the story of the little boy whose optimism exasperated his parents because it made their gloom more glaring. One day, they filled his room with horse manure, believing he would find this finally repulsive. When the boy entered his room, he gleefully concluded: "Oh, there must be a pony here somewhere. I love ponies!"

Midlife has gifted me with an openness. My eyes are more open now to the beauty around me: the flowers, the sun, even the hidden symmetry in that unwanted heap of garbage. Ah, life's irony! My eyesight deteriorates with hyperopia and astigmatism. But why do I see the myriad colors of everyday life more clearly? Maybe because midlife has given them more meaning. They are now testimonies to God's greatness.

My ears are now sensitive to the sound of the wind, the whimper of a child, the melody in the siren of a careening ambulance, the hope in the *puto* vendor's stentorian "*putooooo ... puto kayo riyan*" as it heralds another day, Pete's sigh of relief when I don't work on weekends as against his muted impatience when I overstay in the bathroom.

I can now hear the rhythm of life, from Forbes Park to Tondo, from the chirping of the *maya* to the bell ringing at the Consecration at Mass to the woodsawing of the carpenter to the abused office computer keyboard to the heart-pounding blare at the disco.

The tactility quotient seems greater at midlife, too. Perhaps the sensitivity exercises at those drama workshops have finally rubbed off. After 32 years of marriage, four children and six grandchildren, I still gather electricity from rubbing shoulders with my husband. My baby grandson's cling brings me much reassurance. Steam on my face from the whistling teakettle is doubly refreshing. So is the gentle massage of a hot bath at the end of a busy day. Midlife has, at last, made me sensuous.

Midlife has also given me time. Well, not any more or less than the 24 hours a day that He has given us all. In that sense, time is a great leveler. I meant that midlife has taught me time management, a major component of which is enjoying time without feeling guilty.

Earlier on, I was a veritable slave to time, perhaps an overreaction to the constant admonition in grade school that God will, at the final judgment, demand an accounting of every minute He has given us. Immaturely, I interpreted such as rigidity in the use of time, enough to incite guilt upon leisure or anger when schedules went awry.

Now I no longer panic when I'm late for an appointment if it's not my fault. When I can't make a deadline despite my best efforts, I simply notify and express apology without belaboring explanation. I've begun to learn not to lose sleep over unreached work goals for reasons beyond my ken and my staff's efforts. It suffices that we all did our best. I figure the boss will understand. And if he doesn't, despite reasonable explanation, it's just too bad.

The bottom line is I know I can't please all of the people all of the time. And pleasing people no longer preoccupies me.

Midlife has taught me to complement this, however, with a deep understanding of other people's circumstances. Some call this "compassion" or the capacity to feel with the other, to put oneself in the other's shoes without jeopardizing discipline.

While I still do not have Time in my hands, I now savor every opportunity that the present brings me. There's a lot of wisdom in the banker's adage: "The past is a cancelled check; the future is but a promissory note; the present is like cash – use it fully and spend it wisely before it slips on to yesterday."

There is even greater sense in the motto "Relish the moment," especially when coupled with Psalm 118:24: "This is the day which the Lord has made. Let us be glad and rejoice in it."

The essayist Robert Hastings agrees: "It isn't the burdens of today that drive men mad. It is the regrets over yesterday and the fear of tomorrow. Regret and fear are twin thieves who rob us of today. So stop pacing the aisles and counting the miles. Instead, climb more mountains, eat more ice cream, go barefoot more often, swim more rivers, watch more sunsets, laugh more, cry less. Life must be lived as we go along."

Midlife flexibility transcends time management. It flows into people management — from husband and children to staff and household. We have learned that in addition to compassion cum discipline, a vital tool in management is cementing a foundation in people and "letting them go" afterward. It means liberating them from the mold in which we have cast them, letting them be the best they can and want to be.

Whether it's our children or our protegés we need to "let go" of, Kahlil Gibran, that dear Lebanese poet/philosopher, may strike some sensitive chords with his admonition:

"Your children are not your children.
They are the sons and daughters of Life's longing for itself.
They come through you, but not from you.
And though they are with you, yet they belong not to you.
You may give them your love, but not your thoughts,
for they have their own thoughts.
You may house their bodies, but not their souls,
for their souls dwell in the house of tomorrow
which you cannot visit, not even in your dreams.
You may strive to be like them,
but seek not to make them like you.
For life goes not backward nor tarries with yesterday."

Midlife's final lesson teaches me not just to "let go" but to "let God." The "letting go" comprises the midlifer's selflessness and his daringness to venture into and accept the unknown. The "letting God" is one's ultimate story of tried humility, that which continually acknowledges his nothingness in God's presence, and unwavering faith in the Almighty's power and goodness.

This spawns a paradoxical mix of serenity in faith and restlessness in the desire to serve more fully — found mostly in midlife and stabilized gently by this invocation which we once clipped from an old newspaper and has since been a ready recharger of occasionally flagging spirits:

"Disturb us, Lord,
When with the abundance of things we possess,
we have lost the thirst for the water of life.

When having fallen in love with time,
we have ceased to dream of eternity;

and in our efforts to build the new earth,
have allowed our vision of heaven to grow dim.

Stir us, O Lord, to dare more boldly,
to venture on wider seas,
where storms shall show Thy majesty,
where, in losing sight of land, we shall find the stars.

In the name of Him who pushed back
the horizons of our hope
and invited the brave to follow him."

The Inner Journey

MARIA VICTORIA RUFINO

"My paintings evoke the feelings, moods and memories of a personal odyssey, the search for meaning in life. As I release my spirit to the idyllic realm of dreams, I experience a sense of freedom, a continuing romance with Nature.

"This solitary voyage to distant places mirrors my inner journey to my heart — where time stands still, where silence is an endless song of joy, where colors swirl in celebration of life. I share the poetry and beauty of my world through my dreamscapes, my tribute to Nature."

"Dreamscapes," seventh solo exhibition, 1995

PASSION is the energy that inspires me to create, to paint, to write, to work, to love. It is the vital thread that links the different facets of myself and weaves them into a vibrant, textured tapestry. It injects sparkle and soul into everything I do and feel.

On the brink of midlife, I am exploring new paths and new roles. By experiencing the physical, emotional and spiritual rites of passage, I am gaining wisdom and insight.

Writing about my inner journey is not easy. I consider painting a more satisfying method of expression. Its visual poetry and artistic images may be interpreted subjectively by a viewer.

In contrast, writing prose requires an exact verbalization and communication of thoughts. The writer is open and vulnerable to a reader's objective scrutiny.

MIDLIFE is the pause in a woman's ascent to independence and self-fulfillment. At this plateau, she undergoes a physical, emotional and spiritual transformation. She reflects on all the facets of the first four decades, the passions and drama of living.

By midlife, a woman shall have undergone some of the joy of loving and the pain of letting go.

A few years ago, I was bewildered when a family problem precipitated an early crisis. Although it came at a time when I had finally found a sense of balance and order in my life, I was totally unprepared for it.

Suddenly, things seemed to go beyond my control. I was forced into a situation where I had to make difficult and painful decisions. (In retrospect, I realize now that there was a divine plan, a reason for the upheaval. All I needed to do was to leave it to Heaven and allow things to happen.)

The love between a mother and her son is a pure, intense, exclusive and complex relationship. It defies scientific explanation. Every woman who is a mother would know what it means to love unconditionally.

In adolescence, a growing son undergoes physical and emotional changes that are confusing to both himself and his mother. He begins to assert his independence. To a single part-time mother, an only son's natural desire to stretch his wings seems threatening. Without adequate preparation and effective communication, a rift in the relationship is inevitable.

Although a mother and her son love each other deeply, there are periods when they need time to cool off, to see and appreciate each other — from a safe distance.

An apparently innocent quarrel erupted into a prolonged estrangement. Simmering emotions and long unresolved conflicts came to a head.

I grieved inside me for many months. I took positive steps to regain my balance and perspective. I sought counseling from a trusted psychologist-friend who understood our delicate family situation. I needed to understand the reasons behind this test of separation.

My counselor advised me to let my 18-year-old son go. He needed to be away for a while, to grow up without me. The only assurance I received was that he would return someday — as an adult, and a friend.

That long period of solitude was agonizing. I had to learn to be patient beyond belief. I worried and waited, prayed and lit innumerable candles for 16 months. Beyond prayer, I tapped into an inner reservoir of strength and spirituality.

In the meantime, I sent short notes to my son. No response came except for infrequent, indirect messages and a card.

I masked the emotional upheaval well by plunging deeper into work and obligatory social activities. Time passed. Days blurred into nights and weeks turned into months.

I attended Jungian workshops at the Cenacle Retreat House to explore my psyche. I listened to my subconscious and analyzed my dreams. I learned about the archetypes, the process of individuation, wounding and integration.

At the Cenacle, I met the Oblate Sisters of the Most Holy Redeemer, the nuns who run St. Mary's House for young girls in Tagaytay. I discovered that their special vocation is to heal and rehabilitate the psyches of abused young women.

Focusing on the young girls opened my eyes to the problems of wounded women. Their psychic scars fade only after years of therapy and productive work. To call attention to their plight, I wrote an article on them for publication. That piece on St. Mary's relaunched my writing career.

In a different sense, I was undergoing a cleansing, healing process of my own. The sisters helped me weather the crisis through their prayers.

A few months later, I developed a fever that lingered for a month. During my convalescence, I immersed myself in painting and in spring cleaning—both physical and spiritual. The process of internal and external renovation happened simultaneously.

I began to question the value of being in a career versus the freedom of being on my own. Analyzing my current lifestyle in the context of my demanding work, I realized it was a classic case of burnout.

I had been in a wonderfully challenging job as a hotel executive for eight years. At the same time, I was struggling to be a good visual artist. I divided my time between work and painting. Somewhere in between, during my annual vacation leave, I produced international concerts. As an art management consultant, I helped set up a prestigious annual national student art competition. It was a satisfying setup, or so I thought.

I loved being busy and being involved in a whirl of activities. But the carousel spun too fast for me. The unhealthy work environment with countless events wore me down. I disliked wearing a social mask and dealing with corporate intrigue.

My confinement was a time of spiritual reflection. It led me to the realization that I wanted to be free. I needed to make a drastic change in my career.

I nourished my tired spirit and healed myself through painting.

During this critical time, I tackled a series of major legal exercises. I obtained a US divorce and dissolution of conjugal property. I hurdled the trauma of twin annulments — church and state.

Undergoing the interviews and tedious tests with my canon lawyer, a Jesuit priest, was a catharsis. It was a painful time of remembering, of tears and nightmares. By writing my case history, I was able to release long buried memories and pain.

It was a relief to receive the canonical declaration of nullity from the Matrimonial Tribunal and the confirmation from the Ecclesiastical Tribunal. My life had been returned to me. I felt vindicated.

The state annulment was granted a year later. Compared to the church proceedings, the civil process was less painful. Psychologically, I passed through the flames and emerged with my faith intact.

After receiving the civil annulment, I resolved another significant problem. After weighing the odds, I disengaged myself from a complex relationship. I unloaded all my emotional baggage.

I quit my job and wiped the slate clean.

The beginning of midlife marked a new turning point. It was a chance to begin all over again.

(My first turning point happened in 1982 when I moved to New York to complete my college education. It was one of the most exciting, adventurous episodes in my life. After graduation, I considered several interesting job prospects but I missed my son. I came home the following Christmas, ready to renew our ties. Instead of joining the family business as expected, I pursued a different and more difficult path. I joined the corporate world.)

Now was the time to take a short, creative sabbatical abroad. I traveled extensively and produced two musical concerts in California. I retraced my early meandering, rediscovered old haunts and visited beloved places.

I came to appreciate things in a different light and started sketches for a new series of dreamscapes. The experience was rejuvenating, akin to dipping a faded sepia photo in a technicolor wash of brilliance.

Back home, a blur of holidays and celebrations passed — a solo exhibit, my birthday, Easter, my son's nineteenth birthday, New Year. My son was conspicuously absent except for two hours on Christmas Eve. He appeared for a poignant and brief dinner, only to vanish for several more months.

Although my family and friends surrounded me, someone very important was missing.

I painted on a brave smile.

My next exhibit was a sellout and drew encouraging reviews. Despite my inner anxiety, angst and gloom, my dreamscapes revealed quite the opposite. They evoked serenity and joy. As in the past, art healed me.

He suddenly appeared the day before my birthday, in April 1993. From out of the blue, he called to say "hello." It was as if he had never left. Although he was still a college sophomore, he wanted to produce a play and earn some money. He wanted me to teach him the ropes. We had a tentative first working meeting during which we discussed logistics for the play.

On my birthday, we finally celebrated all the missed occasions over a quiet candlelight dinner and champagne.

I never asked any questions about his absence. He did not offer any explanations. I guess that's what being a mother means — unconditional love. I realized that our bond was never broken. It merely stretched long enough — to accommodate his growing pains.

The play was a big success. My son, as associate producer, donated a big portion of the income to St. Mary's House. He returned to his alma mater that June and paid for his college tuition out of his earnings. My heart burst with pride at the knowledge that he had learned his lessons well.

As my wise mentor had predicted, my son came back a man. He was prepared, and I was ready, to assume our new roles as friends and partners. And we are going through positive transitions together.

Things ran smoothly until he decided to marry two months before his college graduation.

The marriage threw me off balance for a while. It was another phase I had not expected to happen so soon. I had so many dreams for him. He reassured me that he understood the responsibilities of marriage.

With pride, I felt relieved when he finally marched up the stage to receive his diploma. He was now ready to fight his own battles.

I have learned to accept his decision to marry with equanimity and grace. Despite their youth, BR and his wife Michelle seem to be taking the right path. With a little guidance from above, I am confident they will succeed in building a strong, enduring family.

On August 8, an astrologically auspicious date, my first grandchild, Brandon Ryan Frederic, was born. A spitting image of his dad, BRyan is the exquisite angel-child I always longed to have. I feel blessed with this wonderful gift of life. His arrival has made my little family complete.

I am progressing to another phase of maturity. I am fortunate to have been born with age-defying genes. Becoming a grandmother is not as frightening as most women fear. It depends on one's attitude and lifestyle.

I have gone back to another childhood passion — horses. The exercise keeps me young and trim. I eagerly look forward to the time when BRyan and I will ride the wind together.

EVERY WOMAN approaching midlife passes through a phase in which her biological clock reminds her that time is running out. We instinctively make our choices based on natural urges. My inner clock was clanging loudly.

On cue, the free spirit within me mellowed. I have contemplated making a permanent commitment several times. But each time, when plans had to be finalized, I would retreat into the safety of my shell.

My reluctance to commit myself stemmed from my unwillingness to risk alienating my son. He was growing up and needed me. I could not uproot myself and leave him behind. Ironically, he is not aware of the excruciatingly difficult decisions I have made.

Falling in love is the biggest physical thrill imaginable. Chemistry between two individuals is an inexplicable, complex biochemical process. It goes beyond the cerebral, logical side that governs life. Everything shuts down, albeit temporarily. Time stands still. A magical aura surrounds a couple in love.

It is entirely possible for two people to meet, connect and disconnect within an incredible time frame. Like a bolt of lightning or a puff of smoke.

In this incarnation, I have experienced an eclectic medley of unforgettable friendships. Each one has taught me a lesson. I have had my share of roller-coaster rides, of highs and lows, pleasure and pain, angst and disillusionment.

Though a special friendship may not last a lifetime, it is a valid, enriching process of growth. I have learned more about myself as a result of interaction with others. I have acquired a discerning eye with which to see and understand life better.

Social pressure dictates that a woman should not live alone. She should settle down and nest. I tried that route early in life and got badly burned. There have been glamorous, attractive, sophisticated men who seemed to be knights in shining armor. Relying on my intuition and survival instinct, I wisely waited. After the initial sizzle and sparkle of a romance faded, I discovered chinks in the polished exterior, flaws in the apparently perfect coat of arms or rust in the joints.

Once I thought I had found a rare intellectual rapport and a spontaneous sense of humor with a special someone. But the timing was off. I was not ready to live abroad permanently. I decided that a long-distance romance was highly impractical.

A relationship cannot flourish if there are too many obstacles and conflicts, such as a cultural clash or an extreme age gap. The options begin to narrow as a woman matures. She becomes more discriminating and selective.

Divine Providence has saved me from what my spiritual adviser described as "a fate worse than death." Marriage to the wrong partner would be a life sentence without parole.

It would be folly to commit the same mistake twice just to please society or to escape being lonely. Being in love is not the same as sharing compatible interests with someone. I would rather thrive on happy solitude than compromise my hard-earned freedom and identity.

It would be unwise to sublimate myself in a relationship that will stifle my growth. A woman should not give up a part of herself as a sacrificial offering. Giving up herself diminishes her and creates unrealistic expectations.

Through the years, I have discovered profound insights about human nature. I wish I had found these gems in my twenties. Life's funny that way. You have to make mistakes and get hurt first before you acquire wisdom.

Once upon a time, I was a delicately soft, naive and vulnerable girl. I had so many idealistic dreams, so many plans. I took a few detours along the way to find myself. I feel that I am stronger and wiser now. I have passed through several tests of fire.

My heart may be a bit battle-scarred and weary from the effort of loving. But it still beats gently. One day, my soul mate will reappear. When the time is right, things will fall into place.

PLAYING many different roles is very difficult for any woman, no matter how accomplished or competent she is. Anne Morrow Lindbergh, in her inspiring book *Gift from the Sea*, writes that a woman cannot exist indefinitely in a state of fragmentation, *"Zerrisenheit,"* torn-to-pieces-hood. She would be shattered into a thousand pieces in her pursuit of centrifugal activities. A woman who has to be so many things to so many people eventually runs dry.

Mrs. Lindbergh's thoughts resonate with my own. I have found validation in our shared experiences — in a woman's longing for a space of her own, in the symbolism of the sea and the seashells.

Although I want to do so many things and try so many roles, I am beginning to consolidate my energies and focus on the most important priorities.

Women the world over have vastly different cultures and lifestyles yet all our concerns are universal. We all have experienced love and passion, though they come in different packages. At midlife, we all undergo emotional, spiritual and physical changes. How we react to these changes is what ultimately matters.

MY PASSION for painting started in childhood. I enjoyed doodling, drawing, scribbling with watercolors and crayons. Art was the exhilarating outlet for my boundless energy.

The competitive ambiance and academic demands of school took precedence over painting. The desire to paint was sublimated in my pursuit of academic excellence. Although there were sporadic artistic bursts, painting remained dormant throughout marriage and early motherhood.

I realized that a vital dimension within me needed fulfillment. I found peace in the contemplative discipline of painting. Art became a spiritual haven as I passed through life's distressing and turbulent stages. Painting was the only constant source of balance and serenity.

Now, 20 years later, my painting style is slowly evolving and unfolding. The growth process has been painfully slow. It is the result of the demands of multiple responsibilities in diverse professional incarnations. I have been treading parallel paths of dual yet diametrically opposed careers — business and art. And I am still learning the fine art of compromise.

Nine years ago, I mustered the courage to hold my first major exhibition. It was time, my mentor advised, to test the waters. I had participated in several group shows of Oriental art. That was the safe route — going with the crowd.

I wanted to assert myself as an independent painter with a style that merged two influences — East and West. The success of that first show encouraged me to pursue my vocation.

Working in the corporate world and being a weekend painter was a tough balancing act. I had to prioritize my time and energy, split myself into two. The polarities had to coexist.

A venerable art patroness advised me not to give up one for the other. Business, she said, is necessary to keep me balanced.

My job supported my art. I realized that there are advantages to being ambidextrous and multidimensional. It is a matter of using both the left and the right sides of the brain. One needs stamina and determination to withstand the conflicts of opposing energies. In a prolonged tug-of-war, one side eventually caves in.

A confluence of events helped me decide. Although my spirit wanted to prolong the battle, my body could not take the pressures. I got sick for a month. During the enlightening period of convalescence, I painted. And I was happy.

It has been four years since I made the earth-shaking decision to switch careers. The small steps I have taken are tiny when compared to the gigantic strides by other artists. I am slowly plodding along, experimenting with the possibilities in watercolor. The medium is most difficult, demanding and challenging.

However, watercolor suits my temperament best. To the lay person, it may seem easy. Not true. One has to make precise, confident and perfect strokes. There is no room for error. A minute error, a false stroke could destroy the entire painting and ruin its translucent quality. I am a perfectionist in that sense. I demand so much from myself because it is the only way I can improve. When I am painting, I am completely immersed in another dimension.

In the past, I have dabbled in oil, charcoal, pastel, wood, leather, ceramic and stained glass. Trying out the different media gives an aspiring artist the chance to experiment and explore. Watercolor clicked. I toiled for ten years in the Oriental discipline — learning how to control the flow of water and ink, light and shadow, tonal values of black and white. The contemplative effect of painting produced the tranquility I needed.

I learned the Western technique from my guru. He believed in my talent and guided me through the first three exhibitions. When he felt that I could swim on my own, he wisely let go.

My personal style is emerging. Like most artists, I sometimes have doubts about the direction I am taking. But I have to trust my instincts and take risks.

Nature is my eternal muse. I celebrate her perfection in every painting — the sunset, sea, sky, flora and fauna. Even my rare attempts at abstraction are musings on the same theme. Like a symphony of music, my dreamscapes depict variations of images, feelings and ideas.

My artistic side is unfolding. I have achieved my primary goals — to hold an international show and to write a book. The dreams will not stop there. My commitment to art is forever.

Somewhere in the distant future, I hope to devote myself to the arts. I pray fervently for the inspiration and the discipline to persevere despite the odds.

I am in the midst of preparing a new body of works, a collection of paintings that have seen me through the rough times of the past two years. They reflect a changing consciousness and a transforming attitude about my life.

I BELIEVE that things do not happen simply by coincidence. There is always a reason behind every crisis. A problem arises because it will teach us a lesson. We are not given a situation that is impossible to resolve. It takes time and patience. Above all, it takes faith and grace.

Making sense out of the confusing upheavals of midlife is the ultimate challenge to a woman. There are no instant solutions, no formulas for coping. One has to keep growing on all levels, especially the spiritual.

A woman does not have to define herself by a man or by standards set by others. She should seek her place in the sun and adapt to a changing world.

On my part, I am continually striving, not for perfection, but for excellence. I am no longer driven to run at a competitive, frenetic pace to prove myself. I would rather develop myself as a compleat woman and as an artist.

My new career allows me to be flexible, to wear several hats and to try new roles. I have new and fascinating challenges but the pace is more comfortable.

At this point, I am where I want to be. I have independence and the time to be me.

My Life, My Passion, My Hope
Rev. Dr. Elizabeth S. Tapia

Who Am I?

I am a woman. i am brown. i am alive.

i am struggling. i am hoping.

I am passionately in love with life! i am a christian.

i am married. i am a professor/student of theology. i am a lower middle-class professional.

I AM A feminist. I regard sexism, racism and classism as the unholy trinity. I am not a man hater. What I abhor is the oppressive and dominant system in all areas of life and relationships. I try to contribute to the well-being of all, particularly to the least of our sisters and brothers.

I love surprises, especially pleasant ones. I love watching birds, moonshine, ocean waves, sunrises and sunsets. I pray and I am prayed for. Vegetarian meals, herbal teas and any kind of nuts suit my taste. I easily laugh and I cry hard. I sometimes forget names but I remember every kind word or deed someone does to me or to others.

I love myself because God first loved me. So I must be very special! Because I believe in the unconditional love of God, I am challenged to love others, even my enemies or those who have a grudge against me. It is more freeing to love than to hate. It is more blessed to have a passion for life than a passion for death.

I GREW UP in a Bulacan village with two brothers and seven sisters, *Inang* and *Amang*. There was no electricity then, and no dolls to play with, but I did enjoy the *duyan* by a *camachile* tree. There was not much food on the table, either. At an early age I learned to share everything: *baon, payong, kumot, kamote, damit, pagmamahal,* etc.

I am now on my forty-seventh year of living on borrowed time in this world. I joyfully claim my space, worth and dignity. Every morning when I wake up I smile to myself, to the Gracious Spirit and to the *sampaguita* plants outside my window. Then I take a brisk 30-minute walk, followed by Shibashi Tai chi meditation by my small peace garden, and end with a short prayer for peace, loving kindness and justice for all created beings and Mother Earth.

I am an ordained pastor in the United Methodist Church in the Philippines, belonging to the Bulacan Annual Conference. I was ordained in 1976 when not too many women in the Protestant churches were being ordained. It was a struggle. While there are some Protestant churches that accept and practise ordination of women, many still think it is against Christian faith and doctrine. The patriarchal theology that says "only men can be priests or pastors" and that "women should be silent in the church" must be thrown out the window. I strongly believe that the church will be a viable force for change in the twenty-first century when it becomes fully just, prophetic, creative, inclusive, participatory, healthy and joyful.

Yes, there is sexism even in church and the mustard seed that fires me up is the vision of shalom. This vision of shalom is a vision for wholeness and health, abundant life and harmony. When Jesus said, "I came that you may have life and have it abundantly" (John 10:10), he pronounced the gospel of shalom, of salvific and life-giving relationship in all its dimensions. But do the majority of our people experience abundant life? Do the majority of women in church and society enjoy a discrimination-free zone? Why do women continue to suffer violence (physical, emotional, etc.), subjugation and oppression? Why do men preach while women bleach? Why do women pastors and deaconesses receive smaller salaries than male pastors? Why do many refer to God only as "He" and would think of God as male? Why not take our language for God, our theology, in symbolic terms rather than in literal and absolute terms?

In 1974, I began my theological studies at the Pacific School of Religion in Berkeley, California. My conservative theology and moralistic stance were challenged. The brewing student radicalism and growing feminism in the West shocked me. The cultural diversities of the Bay Area appealed to me. I felt very homesick, too, for my family, for the Philippines, for *adobo, mangga* and the Philippine brand of Christmas. Immediately after my graduation and ordination, I returned to Manila to teach at Harris Memorial College, the Development Center for Women.

In 1991, I joined the faculty of Union Theological Seminary in Dasmariñas, Cavite. There I handle the courses of systematic theology, feminist theology, philosophy of religion, Third World liberation theologies. If in the past women were made invisible in theology and history, nowadays they are doing theology and writing their own herstories. Churches and communities are richer when they acknowledge and tap the talents, gifts and presence of women.

What are my passions in my forties?

I have a passion to be alive and healthy. In 1992, I underwent major surgery to remove several myomas around my uterus. Before that, I had lumps in one breast removed, and I thought of my aunt who died of breast cancer. I became anxious about my health and survival. Then a big bonus: no sign of malignancy. The following New Year, I resolved to do self-examination, have a pap smear and medical check-ups regularly, avoid pork and fatty food, eat lots of fruits and vegetables, de-stress, exercise, do positive thinking, avoid negative people, meditate, and learn to express anger and forgiveness.

I have a passion to learn. There is so much to learn even in my mid-forties. Learning from the life stories of women in the Philippines and in Asia and how they do theology in their particular contexts is truly inspiring. Due to ecumenical involvements, I have had the privilege of traveling to many parts of the world and learning from other cultures. It is a humbling and gratifying experience. For instance, in 1994 in Cameroun, Africa, our ecumenical group was graciously hosted by Christian women. At the reception on opening night, many of the women were dancing, singing and smiling. But I noticed an older woman just sitting in a corner. Why was she not dancing and having fun? Did she resent our presence? I found out later through an interpreter that this lady, who came from a rural area, had waited the whole day for a bus, then walked for four hours under the hot sun so she could attend the reception. When she finally arrived at the place, she could barely move her feet, much less dance. From her I learned lessons of perseverance, genuine hospitality and warm sisterhood.

I have a passion for teaching. Be it a formal class, a seminar, or a Bible study under a mango tree, I do enjoy teaching because I am challenged to learn more in my field. It is inspiring to see the faces of young people eager to learn and to share.

I have a passion for justice, peace and integrity of creation. I believe human beings are capable of being justicemakers and peacelovers. In a world of violence, chaos, destruction and greed, we need more love, we need a passion for justice, peace and integrity of creation. Let us teach peace, not violence. At a wedding I co-officiated before Christmas, the newlyweds, Darlene and Joey, gave plant seedlings to every guest at their reception. I liked that very much!

I have a passion to admit mistakes and to say sorry. When I was younger, I found it hard to admit mistakes and even harder to say "I'm sorry." Pride got in the way and I am sorry about that. Now that I am older and a bit wiser, I am no longer afraid to ask questions. Where I have committed wrong or made mistakes, I find people to be understanding and accommodating. To love means to be able to say sorry sincerely.

I have a passion for love and spiritual connection. I was 38 when I married Alan. It was not physical attraction at first sight, but for me a spiritual connection. We became friends, then prayer partners, then lovers (we still are!), then married partners. I am overwhelmed by his love for me. He respects me and supports my vocation. We share the ups and downs of an interracial marriage and cross-cultural relationships. And I love him dearly, especially when he calls me *"Giliw"* or *"Sinta."* We do many things together joyfully: cooking, jogging, eating, praying, making love, teaching, watching sunsets, riding buses, meditation, swimming, traveling and more. I feel very much connected spiritually not only to my spouse but also to my friends (women and men, married or single, heterosexual or lesbian/gay) and prayer partners around the world. God to me is the encompassing and empowering Spirit of Love, Understanding, Harmony and Peace. God dwells in us; God breathes in Life. And I am committed to practise this God-given life to overcome death-dealing forces.

I have a passion for Asian women's theology. In the last 20 years, Asian Christian women's theologies have emerged. Women in Asia are reflecting on their life experiences and struggles in the light of their faith and contexts. Feminist theology in Asia is vibrant, creative, action-oriented, community-centered, ecologically sensitive, liturgical and practical.

Women's theology in the Philippines is a theology of struggle and hope. As women aim for personal and societal wholeness, they are giving birth to hope, a hope that steers them toward self-confidence, social justice, freedom and solidarity. For example, my friend Jane, who joined the underground movement during the martial-law years, once told me that a concrete expression of one's belief in God is serving the people. She understands God as the "power within the people as they participate in achieving freedom, peace and justice everywhere."

I DRAW strength and inspiration from many sources: a sense of calling and commitment; the wellspring of love and support from Alan Dale, my partner in ministry and marriage; my family, close friends, prayer partners, guardian angels, including my late mother, faith in Jesus Christ, the feminist movement, beautiful and laughter-full nieces and nephews, going to the beach to swim and meditate, going to Silang market, picking vegetables from our garden, doing Shibashi Tai chi meditation; visits with Sr. Mary John Mananzan and other friends at the Institute of Women's Studies in Manila; friends and coworkers in the United Methodist Church, my students and colleagues at Union Theological Seminary in Dasmariñas; Deena, our faithful dog, and Pasa, our curious cat. I feel and receive *prana* (life-energy) from the surrounding trees and plants, from the grass, and the fresh and cool air coming from Silang, Cavite, and Tagaytay. I gratefully receive many blessings from God the Creator, Redeemer and Sustainer.

Now and tomorrow I hope and dream that there will be no more wars, no more sexual and domestic violence; that there will be harmony and justice in all relations; that human rights, especially those of children, women and the indigenous peoples all over the world will be respected and upheld; that there will be a vegetable garden in every home, and a school and a health center in every barrio; jobs for those who are in need, and a vacation for those who are ready; no more prisons and drug rehabilitation centers and women refuge centers because we shall no longer need them; ordination for Roman Catholic, Jewish and Protestant women who want it and are trained for it; a violence-free world and a pollution-free environment; crises that can be turned into opportunities; a true spirit of ecumenism and solidarity; lower prices for rice and other commodities; the *bayanihan* spirit rather than the "*talangka*" mentality; an end to the traffic mess in Manila.

I want to learn to speak and write in Spanish, Swedish, Ilocano and Hebrew; to be able to adopt a girl who needs a home and who will also adopt me and Alan as her parents; to write and publish a book on theology before I turn 50; to meet Nelson Mandela, Aung Sang Suu Kyi and the Dalai Lama in person, and to be able to taste their courage, faith and determination; to be a friend to the HIV-positive and persons with AIDS. And I want my church to elect a woman bishop.

I have simple wishes as well: to get a telephone at home, to vacation in Sagada and see the rice terraces, to share rice with the hungry, to live fully and to die peacefully.

Let me conclude with this prayer-poem:

Blessed are You, O God, who gave me the gift of life,
of breath, of a divine image in my womanist body.
Blessed are You, O Gracious and Compassionate Spirit, who
provide wisdom and compassion to believing women and men regardless
of color, creed, contexts and choices.
Fill the earth with love and peace, kindness and wholeness.
Fill my midlife years with passion and compassion.
Empty my heart of unhealthy emotions
and fill it with energizing ones.
Lead me to the paths of righteousness, openness, justice,
spirituality, sensuality and childlike joy!
Open my eyes to see the needy and the exploited,
And when I see them, to be an advocate for them and to struggle with them.
Bless my dreams, hopes, passions; bless my body and mind as well.
Bless Mother Earth and all that is within her and around her.
You are Holy, Oh God, You are One. You are beyond me and
within me. Blessed be Your name.
You created us human beings, male and female in Your image.
As we celebrate life in the midst of life's uncertainty,
bless our lives with shalom and genuine security.
We are alive! We are struggling.
We are hoping. We are women in midlife passion,
With fire in our bellies and compassion deep within we
can change the world.
So be it.

She has been the recipient of the following awards: Woman of Distinction from Soroptimist International of Makati, Woman of the Year from *Perspectives* publication of the Catholic Educators Association of the Philippines, Mariang Maya from the Sigma Delta Phi Alumnae Association and a professional award in economics from the UP Alumni Association.

She and her husband Christian have five children.

CRISTINA JAYME MONTIEL is an associate professor in the psychology department of the Ateneo de Manila University and a research fellow at the university's Center for Social Policy and Public Affairs.

She has an A.B. in sociology (cum laude) from Maryknoll College, a master's in psychology from the Ateneo and a Ph.D. in social psychology, also from the Ateneo. She attended a training program in quantitative methods of social research at the Center for Political Studies, Institute for Social Research, of the University of Michigan.

She has had academic visits to the University of Hawaii, the Australian National University, Xiamen University in the People's Republic of China, and the Technische Universitate Chemnitz-Zwickau in Germany. Her latest academic visit, scheduled this spring, is to Ohio State University.

She is currently doing collaborative research on the ethics of international development aid with the psychology department of Laurentian University in Ontario, Canada. Her other professional activities include being cochair of the Conflict Resolution Working Group of the American Psychological Association's Division of Peace Psychology, editorial board member of Peace and Conflict: Journal of Peace Psychology of the American Psychological Association, and member of the scientific program committee for the 1998 Convention of the International Association of Applied Psychology's Division of Political Psychology.

Her teaching expertise lies in the areas of political psychology, psychology of peace and violence, and research methods. She has published papers in professional publications here and abroad.

During the Marcos dictatorship, she chaired Lingap Bilanggo, a movement for human rights and general amnesty for political prisoners. She has worked as a consultant for training and research at the office of the presidential adviser for the peace process, and as part of the technical staff of the sectoral representative for the fisherfolk.

Since 1982, she has been a core member of the Pilipino Democratic Party's political institute and education committee.

She has a son, Andres, nicknamed Andoy.

MARIA ELISA "Boots" ANSON ROA has been a film, television and stage actress for more than 30 years now. Since early 1996, she has also been vice president of the television division of Premiere Entertainment Productions, Inc.

She majored in speech and drama at the University of the Philippines after graduating with honors from Assumption Convent. While living and working in the United States, she took certificate courses in basic journalism, public and media relations, typing and computer studies and banking.

Besides being a multiawarded actress, she has distinguished herself in other fields. For four years in the Eighties, she served at the Philippine Embassy in Washington, D.C. as press attache, cultural officer and special assistant to the ambassador for media, community and cultural affairs. Following that stint in the foreign service, she worked in various US companies, in positions ranging from bank marketing officer to guest services officer at a hotel to newspaper columnist/feature writer.

Since returning to Manila in 1993, she has resumed her acting career and hosted several television shows. She is also a contributor to the Saturday Special section of the *Philippine Daily Inquirer*. Outside of show business, she is chair of Friends of the Philippine High School for the Arts, vice chair of the National Commission for Culture and the Art's film committee, director of the UP Arts and Letters Alumni Foundation, trustee of Balikatan sa Kaunlaran and editor in chief of the *Balikatan News Herald*, trustee of the Movie Workers Welfare Association, steering committee member of Piso para sa Pasig Movement, director of the Organ Transplant Foundation of the National Kidney Institute, and convenor-couple (with her husband Pete) of the Department of Health-NGO Natural Family Planning Council.

Among the numerous awards she has received are a TOWNS (Ten Outstanding Women in the Nation's Service) award, Gintong Ina from the Gintong Ina Foundation, Outstanding Woman in Media Award from the Philippine Women's University and a Women Who Make a Difference award from Soroptimist International.

The Roas have four children — Lea, Joey, Chiqui and Benjo — and six grandchildren.

MARIA VICTORIA RUFINO is a visual artist who has held nine successful exhibitions of her watercolor Dreamscapes since 1976. She is also a businessperson: chair of LR Consultancy Corporation; director of Mercedes Realty Development Corp. and Rufson Enterprises, Inc., vice president of House of Rafana, Inc., all of them family-owned companies involved in real estate development and management. Besides these, she curates annual exhibits at the Art Corner of the Rufino Pacific Tower.

As executive director of Maverick Productions, she has coproduced stage plays and pop musical concerts in the Philippines, Hong Kong, Italy and the United States.

She finished high school at the Marymount International Schools in Barcelona and Rome, graduating as valedictorian. She is a Liberal Arts honor graduate, major in theatre arts and English literature, of Marymount Manhattan College in New York. She was a member of the National Honors Society of America and the Mother Butler Honors Society. She also attended master classes in drama and modern ballet at the Women's Experimental Theatre and the Martha Graham School of Contemporary Dance in New York. She has participated in special workshops at the Carl G. Jung Institute in San Francisco.

A regular columnist of *Business World*, she launched her first book, *Beyond Brushstrokes*, in 1995. She has written feature articles on life, art and culture for various publications in Manila and New York.

Before striking out on her own, she was public relations director and business development, special events and banquet manager of a Makati hotel. There she was responsible for establishing, managing and curating the Artist's Corner which exhibited shows of famous artists as well as of upcoming handicapped painters for civic and charitable organizations.

A member of the Cheese Club of the Philippines, she enjoys international gourmet cuisine — next to her passions for the visual and performing arts and for riding horses.

She has one son, BR, and a grandson, BRyan.

REV. DR. ELIZABETH S. TAPIA is a full-time professor of systematic theology and feminist theology at Union Theological Seminary. She is also a part-time lecturer at the Institute of Women's Studies of St. Scholastica's College in Manila.

She has a doctorate in religion from Claremont Graduate School in California. She earned her Bachelor of Arts and Bachelor of Christian Education degrees at Harris Memorial College in Manila and her two masteral degrees — in religion and divinity — in the US.

She is a member of the Working Group on Women of the World Council of Churches, the Association of Women in Theology and the Ecumenical Association of Third World Theologians. She has attended various conferences here and abroad as either resource person or participant.

Born and raised in a village in Bulacan, Bulacan, she is married to Alan D. Cogswell, an American teacher and pranic healer. She lists her interests as feminist theology, traveling, reading, poetry, collecting postcards and watching the sunset.

The Editor

LORNA KALAW-TIROL, who turned 50 this year, has been a journalist since 1968.

Her first newspaper job, after graduation from St. Theresa's College and a year of teaching high school students, was as a deskperson at *The Manila Chronicle*. From there she moved on to other jobs at other publications, notably as associate editor of *Asia-Philippines Leader*, *Philippine Panorama* and the post-EDSA *Manila Chronicle*, and editor of *Sunday Inquirer Magazine*. As a freelance journalist during her children's formative years, she wrote columns and feature articles in various magazines. Until recently she had a column called Lives and Times in *The Manila Times*.

Since conceptualizing and editing *Coming to Terms*, which won the Manila Critics Circle's National Book Award for best anthology for 1994, she has developed an interest in creating books. Besides *Women on Fire*, she has two other titles for Anvil this year: *Primed for Life*, a collection of men's writings on midlife, and *Public Faces, Private Lives*, an anthology of her personality profiles. She is also editing *The World of 1896*, a book project of the Ateneo de Manila University. In 1996, she edited the two-volume *Duet for EDSA*, a publication of the Foundation for Worldwide People Power.

She is a board member of the Philippine Center for Investigative Journalism, which she helped found, and of the Policy Review and Editorial Services, Women's Feature Service and Crossroads Publications, Inc.

She is proudest, though, of being *Inay* to her and her husband Vic's two sons, Jo-Ed and Paulo.

The Book Designer

Annaleah (Ani) V. Habúlan has been editorial assistant and production coordinator of Anvil Publishing since 1993. She moonlights as a book designer, writer and translator.

She has an A.B. journalism degree from the Faculty of Arts and Letters of the University of Santo Tomas where she edited the art and culture section of the university paper, *The Varsitarian*.

She wants to write her own books for children and a volume she is tentatively calling *Working with Writers and Artists*. The latter will be a tribute to two of the most influential groups of people in her life.

The Writers

MARILEN ABESAMIS attended St. Theresa's College, the University of the Philippines Institute (now College) of Mass Communication and the New School for Social Research in New York City.

She worked briefly for the *Sunday Times Magazine* of *The Manila Times* after graduation from UP, then at *The New York Times,* and edited several company publications in New York and San Francisco.

In Mindanao, she cofounded the Alternative Forum for Research in Mindanao (AFRIM). In San Francisco, she cofounded the Philippine Assistance for Technology and Health (PATH) and edited various expatriate community newsletters.

She lives in Quezon City with her two children, Ami and Anna, and her husband, Walden Bello.

BARBARA C. GONZALEZ has been president of the advertising firm J. Romero & Associates since April 1993. Before that, she was for almost two years chair and president of Coca-Cola Foundation Philippines, Inc. and corporate communications manager of Coca-Cola Bottlers Philippines, Inc.

She was for two years general manager of *The Manila Chronicle,* where she also wrote both opinion and lifestyle columns; before that, vice president, and earlier, management supervisor and account director, of McCann Erickson; division sales manager for Metro Manila and Northern Luzon of Avon Cosmetics, Philippines; vice president for creative services of Avellana & Associates Inc. where she started as a copywriter. While living for two years in the United States in the Eighties, she worked at various jobs, the last one as vice president for marketing and public relations and corporate secretary of F.R.E.E. Management Corporation.

She received her elementary and high school education at Maryknoll College, and from there went to San Jose de Cluny (a Sorbonne affiliate) in Madrid, Spain, for an associate in languages degree; and to Institution Chateau Mont-Choisi in Lausanne, Switzerland. In 1982, she attended the Senior Executive Program for an M.B.A. at the Ateneo Graduate School of Business.

Her book *How Do You Know Your Pearls Are Real?,* a collection of essays published by Anvil, won a National Book Award for 1991 from the Manila Critics Circle.

She has cohosted three television shows: "Times Four," "*Sagot Ko Bayan Ko,*" and "Cafe Bravo."

She is a trustee of the Coca-Cola Foundation Philippines, Inc., director of the Advertising Board of the Philippines and member of the Management Association of the Philippines.

She writes a Sunday column, Reality Check, in the *Philippine Daily Inquirer.*

She has three daughters and one son and is proud to say she is a grandmother.

KATRINA LEGARDA is a partner at the law office Villamor Legarda & Associates and president of LR Consultancy Corporation.

She was educated in England — high school at the Notre Dame Convent at Oxford, and college (B.A. Honors) at the University of Bristol where she majored in history — and returned to the Philippines for law studies at the University of the Philippines. She was admitted to the Philippine bar in 1981.

Starting as an associate at the Angara Abello Concepcion Regala & Cruz Law Office (ACCRALAW) in 1981, she was a partner by the time she left the firm in 1992. While with ACCRALAW, she became known for her defense of journalists Max Soliven and Luis Beltran in the libel suit filed against them by President Corazon Aquino.

She is a member of the Integrated Bar of the Philippines, Rotary Club (Paseo de Roxas, Makati chapter), the UP honors society Order of the Purple Feather, Portia Sorority, Women in Law, Women Lawyers Circle, Iota Tau Tau International Legal Sorority, Circle of Saint Anthony and the Cheese Club of the Philippines. She is a founding member of the Nursing Mothers Association of the Philippines.

She has three children: Jose Primo, Rafael Ramon and Maria Elena Beatriz.

NARZALINA "Narz" ZALDIVAR LIM completed her Bachelor of Arts, major in English literature, at Maryknoll College and her Master of Arts in English at the University of California at Santa Barbara.

She was appointed undersecretary of tourism by President Corazon Aquino in March 1986 and later on as secretary of tourism. She remained in the post until October 1992.

In March 1995, she founded the Asia Pacific Tourism Training Institute, a private tourism training school located in Quezon City, which she herself runs and where she indulges in one of her favorite activities, teaching.

She continues to be involved in various causes. In 1993, she founded Citizens Action Against Crime, a citizens group which has been advocating reforms in the criminal justice system. She still occasionally organizes protest rallies on issues pertaining to peace and order.

She writes an occasional column in a business paper and is often invited to speak at international fora on culture, tourism and the environment.

JULIE LLUCH is the foremost exponent of clay or terra cotta sculpture in the Philippines today. Her highly personal art finds perfect expression in this indigenous and most "sensuous and pleasurable medium." Her ideologically informed works of sculpted women performing various domestic chores are sharp feminist commentary on the circumstances of women's lives. Her later works deal with spiritual themes, particularly the Christian paradox of death and rebirth.

At the forefront of the national women's movement in the area of culture and the arts, she helped form the feminist group Kalayaan together with other women writers and intellectuals in 1983. In 1990 she cofounded Kasibulan, an organization of women visual artists. At present she heads the Philippine Women Artists Collective.

She finished her Bachelor of Philosophy at the College of Philosophy and Letters of the University of Santo Tomas.

She has three daughters: filmmaker Issa and visual artists Aba and Krista.

BABETH LOLARGA is a journalism graduate of the University of the Philippines. Author of two poetry collections, *The First Eye* and *dangling doll: poems of laughter & desperation*, she also coedited the anthology *Telling Lives: Essays by Filipino Women.*

She recently returned to Manila after having lived in Baguio City with her family for a few years, during which she shuttled between a weekday, workaday home and a weekend hideaway. She now works at Raya Media Services, Inc., an advocacy outfit.

SYLVIA L. MAYUGA is an essayist, scriptwriter, occasional poet and filmmaker, and passionate environmentalist.

She has been a columnist in leading dailies, a media consultant, associate editor of various magazines and resident writer of foundations. She is the author of the following books: *Spy in my Own Country* (essays),

Earth Fire and Air (essays), *Encounter with Paradise* (travelogue) and *Journey to the Center* (a monograph on Philippine cultural history).

She has collaborated as writer, director or producer in documentary films and videos on Philippine socio-historical-ecological-cultural topics such as *People Power: the Philippine Experience, In the Ring of Fire and Diptiko.*

She obtained her A.B. in journalism (cum laude) from St. Theresa's College, Manila, and her MS in comparative journalism from Columbia University School of Journalism.

She has been the recipient of the Focus Award, the Golden Quill Award, a National Critics Circle Award, a Catholic Mass Media Award (twice) and a National Book Award.

For several years now, she has been at the forefront of two nongovernmental organizations working to save Mt. Banahaw.

Her only child, Aya, is a gifted young musician.

SOLITA "Winnie" COLLAS-MONSOD enjoys international stature as an expert in economic development econometrics and the multisectoral aspects of development planning, policymaking and implementation. She is well known for her holistic perspective in analyzing development issues, a result of her academic background, experience in government administration and continuing collaboration with development institutions at the local, national, regional and international levels.

She earned her bachelor's and master's degrees in economics at the University of the Philippines and completed all the requirements, except her dissertation, for a doctorate in economics at the University of Pennsylvania.

She was minister (later secretary) of economic planning and concurrently director-general of the National Economic and Development Authority for four years during the Aquino administration.

She is a professor at the UP School of Economics, convenor and chair of the Human Development Network, member of the People's Fact-Finding Committee on Agrarian Reform, adviser of the UP Economics Society, and board member of the Fellows of the Asia Foundation, Batibot Children's Television, Claro M. Recto Memorial Foundation and Social Housing Foundation. She also writes a column in *Business World.*

At the international level, she is a member of the following: the board of trustees of the International Food Policy Research Institute in Washington, D.C., the board of advisors of the South Centre in Geneva, the United Nations Committee for Development Planning and the Regional Poverty Alleviation Group.